BROOKLYN'S BEST

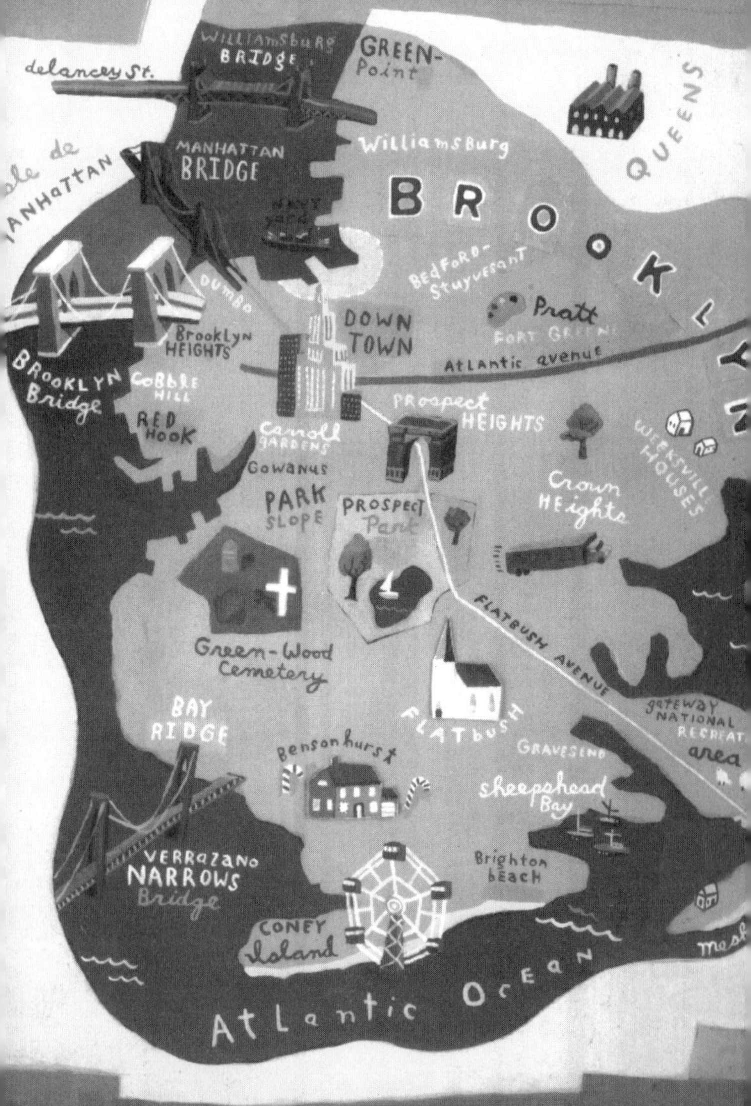
WILLIAMSBURG BRIDGE
delancey St.
GREEN-Point
QUEENS
MANHATTAN BRIDGE
Williamsburg
BROOKLYN
NAVY yard
DUMBO
Bedford-Stuyvesant
Pratt
FORT GREENE
DOWN TOWN
Brooklyn HEIGHTS
Atlantic avenue
BROOKLYN Bridge
COBBLE HILL
RED HOOK
Carroll GARDENS
PROSPECT HEIGHTS
WEEKSVILLE HOUSES
Gowanus
Crown HEights
PARK SLOPE
PROSPECT Park
FLATBUSH AVENUE
Green-Wood Cemetery
BAY RIDGE
FLATBUSH
gateway NATIONAL RECREATION area
GRAVESEND
Bensonhurst
sheepshead Bay
VERRAZANO NARROWS Bridge
Brighton beach
CONEY Island
Atlantic Ocean

BROOKLYN'S BEST

*Sightseeing, Shopping,
Eating, and Happy Wandering
in the Borough of Kings*

ALFRED GINGOLD & HELEN ROGAN

Illustrations by Aaron Meshon

CITY & COMPANY ★ NEW YORK

For our far-flung family—
Jenny and Martin, Judy and David, Harriet
and Sam—and for Toby, our local hero

Copyright © 1998 by Pearl Productions, Inc.

Illustrations © 1998 by Aaron Meshon

All rights reserved. No portion of this book may be reproduced without written permission from the publisher.

Design of cover and text of *Brooklyn's Best*

Copyright © 1998 by Leah Lococo

Library of Congress Cataloging-in-Publication Data

Gingold, Alfred & Rogan, Helen

Brooklyn's best: sightseeing, shopping, eating, and happy wandering in the borough of kings/Alfred Gingold & Helen Rogan.

p. cm.

Includes index.

ISBN1-885492-65-0

1. Brooklyn (New York, N.Y.)—Guidebooks. 2. New York (N.Y.)—Guidebooks.

I. Helen Rogan. II. Title.

F129.87G48 1998

917.47'230443—dc21

98-30502

CIP

First Printing

Publisher's Note: Neither City & Company nor the authors have any interest, financial or personal, in the locations listed in this book. No fees were paid or services rendered in exchange for inclusion in these pages.

CONTENTS

Introduction   9

★

OUR BRIDGE   *12*

★

"To the Tune of Flutes": **BARGEMUSIC**   *14*

★

Brooklyn Holds Its Liquor: **BARS**   *16*

★

Oh Little Town of **BENSONHURST!**   *18*

★

The **BLACK CHURCHES OF BROOKLYN:**
A Visit to Concord Baptist Church of Christ   *19*

★

*The Russians Have Come, The Russians Have
Come!:* **BRIGHTON BEACH**   *22*

★

The Principality of Lichtenstein: **BROOKLYN
ACADEMY OF MUSIC**   *25*

★

The Flowers that Bloom in the Spring:
BROOKLYN BOTANIC GARDEN   *27*

★

BROOKLYN CELEBRATES BIG-TIME:
*You Gotta Have . . . Welcome Back . . . Celebrate . . .
Atlantic Antic . . . aargh! (A User's Guide)*   *29*

★

BROOKLYN CELEBRATES LOCALLY:
Let Us Count the Ways   *31*

★

Walking through History:
BROOKLYN HEIGHTS   *34*

★

For Art's Sake: **BROOKLYN MUSEUM
OF ART**   *36*

Down to the Sea in Ships:
BROOKLYN NAVY YARD   39

★

Moonstruck Brooklyn:
CARROLL GARDENS   42

★

Yes, It Can Be Done! CLOTHES
SHOPPING in Brooklyn   45

★

CONEY ISLAND of the Mind   47

★

Busy Hands: CRAFTS SHOPS and Studios   49

★

DUMBO: See It While You Can   52

★

Dueling DUTCH HOUSES: If You Can't
Choose Which One to See, See 'em All!   53

★

Brooklyn EATS I: The Institutions   56

★

Brooklyn EATS II: Cutting-Edge Cuisine   59

★

Brooklyn EATS III: Ethnic Food   62

★

Go Fish: Brooklyn FISHING Spots   65

★

Ah, FLATBUSH!   68

★

Fabulous FLOYD BENNETT FIELD   71

★

FUNKY FUN: Buzz-a-rama 500, Gil Hodges
Lanes, Brownstone Billiards   73

★

The Dead Really Do Know Brooklyn:
GREEN-WOOD CEMETERY   75

The Brooklyn HEIGHTS PROMENADE:
You Say Promenade, I Say Esplanade
(Both Are Correct!)   78

★

Come On-A My House: The HOUSE TOURS   80

★

Brooklyn Is for KIDS: The Rolodex   83

★

LOOKING FOR TREASURE:
Where to Find Antiques, Almost-Antiques,
and Trendy Knickknacks   91

★

A Tree Grows in Brooklyn—In Fact, Many Do:
MAGNOLIA TREE EARTH CENTER   94

★

Beyond the Biggies:
Brooklyn's Little MUSEUMS   95

★

Waterworld: NEW YORK AQUARIUM
(It's Better Than the Movie)   98

★

We Love the NIGHT LIFE, We Gotta Boogie:
Brooklyn Gets Down   100

★

ONLY IN BROOKLYN:
You Can't Make This Stuff Up   102

★

PALATIAL INSTITUTIONS: The Williamsburgh Savings Bank Tower and Others   105

★

Attention, PARK SLOPE Shoppers!   107

★

The Power of Pratt: The Engine Room
at PRATT INSTITUTE   111

Not Forgotten: The PRISON SHIP MARTYRS'
MONUMENT, *Fort Greene Park* 113

★

Splendor in the Grass: PROSPECT PARK 115

★

RAILROAD MADNESS:
*Atlantic Avenue Tunnel, Broadway Junction,
and Train World* 118

★

RED HOOK'S *Resurrection* 121

★

Earthly Delights: SAHADI IMPORTING
COMPANY, INC. 125

★

He Did Windows: TIFFANY *in Brooklyn* 127

★

A Coffee Shop for All Seasons:
TOM'S RESTAURANT 129

★

Spanning the Narrows: The VERRAZANO-
NARROWS BRIDGE 131

★

High Ideals, Low Rents: WARREN PLACE *and
Other Housing by Alfred Tredway White* 134

★

Ghost Village: WEEKSVILLE HOUSES 135

★

The Artists Have Arrived:
WILLIAMSBURG 137

★

THE ENTHUSIASTS: *People Who Will
Help You Find Out More about Brooklyn* 140

★

Neighborhood Index 148

★

General Index 153

Introduction

"It'd take a guy a lifetime to know Brooklyn t'roo and t'roo. An' even den, yuh wouldn't know it all."
— Thomas Wolfe, *Only the Dead Know Brooklyn*

ONE HUNDRED YEARS after Brooklyn unwillingly merged its identity with that of New York City, Brooklyn is the place to be. People from all over the world come to live here, or just to look—we even have tour buses rumbling up and down our streets. The movies have discovered Brooklyn, too. Native son Spike Lee makes most of his films here, and the borough appears in movies as varied as *The Age of Innocence* (the ball in the brownstone), *Scent of a Woman* (the wild Ferrari ride), and *As Good As It Gets* (Helen Hunt's apartment). These days, the name that for so long evoked a rather narrow vein of nostalgia—the Dodgers and Ebbets Field, egg creams and stickball—means change, hope, style. All around there's activity: new buildings, new jobs, and new talk of great things.

A big, spiffy hotel in downtown Brooklyn? It's happened.

A baseball team in Coney Island? It's going to happen!

A cleanup of the Gowanus Canal?

Well, they're trying. . . .

The funny thing is that despite all the hubbub, Brooklyn remains fundamentally the same. It retains an aura that the world has come to know and love, often without much sense of the real place. This is because

New York City upstages its individual boroughs, and to most of the world, "New York City" means Manhattan. But Brooklyn is too prodigious a place to be treated as a footnote  to that dinky island in the middle of the river.

For three hundred years, Brooklyn has been a magnet for immigrants, and there is no end in sight. Today's Brooklynites are a vibrant mix, representing 93 different ethnic groups. Thousands of Russians, Chinese, Mexicans, Koreans, and Orthodox Jews are making homes and revitalizing neighborhoods. There are professionals doing the brownstone thing with their babies and there are the deeply hip, in their black duds and ear cuffs, boldly going where no bourgeoisie have gone before—as of now, Williamsburg's Northside. And there are the authors of this book, who came to Brooklyn as outlanders—Helen from London, Alfred from Manhattan—and became exhilarated by the experience of living here.

Why do we all love it so? Partly, it's the contradictions. Brooklyn is huge on the map, and it feels even bigger on the ground—miles and miles of low buildings and sky. But that vast area is all neighborhoods, which are tight-knit, proud, and full of character. Brooklyn is a gritty, streetwise burg, but it's also a precinct of tree-lined streets, old row houses, and lovingly tended gardens. Pheasants live out on the abandoned piers of Bush Terminal. Sit out on a stoop on a quiet summer evening, and you can feel a pastoral innocence in the air that harks back to the rural past, the days of the Dutch farmers whose gravestones still survive in the churchyards of Flatbush and Gravesend.

You can sense Brooklyn's ghosts, too. There's room for them to flourish here, and they do—think how many posters of the '55 Dodgers you see in the service stations. But there are others: at the storefront at Livonia and Saratoga Avenues that was headquarters of the notorious Murder, Inc., at the derelict eighteenth-century farmhouse under the MacDonald Avenue el, at the second-floor dance studio in Park Slope where the Persuasions used to practice, in the simple Clinton Hill house where Walt Whitman finished *Leaves of Grass*.

In the course of our research we've discovered a lot about Brooklyn, but some of its mysteries remain:

* How many martyrs are buried beneath the Martyrs' Monument in Fort Greene?
* What exactly are the precise boundaries of Flatbush?
* Is there any way to beat the rush-hour traffic on the Gowanus?
* Why aren't there more good restaurants in the Heights?
* Are all the crock-pots and cruets and Santana albums on offer at Park Slope's innumerable stoop sales actually just a *few* crock-pots and cruets and Santana albums, bought and sold and bought again in an endless cycle of capitalism?
* Kensington, Prospect-Lefferts Gardens, Farragut—are they parts of Flatbush or what?

Come visit, solve your own mysteries, but don't kid yourself that you'll ever know the place like the back of your hand. We suspect that Brooklyn is, as Thomas Wolfe says, ultimately unknowable. Nothing beats trying, though.

Note to the user: *Phone numbers and addresses are liable to change at any time, so* please *check before you go out in order to avoid heartbreak and tears.*

OUR BRIDGE

Any Brooklynite feels a great easing of the soul when crossing the Brooklyn Bridge—especially if the exit to the Brooklyn-Queens Expressway isn't too backed up. Like Stonehenge and the Pyramids, it is an engineering marvel that is also a spiritual emblem of its homeland. Unlike the first two, however, the Bridge is still very much in use. Arguably the most famous bridge in the world and unarguably one of the most beautiful, the Brooklyn Bridge works for a living.

To be best appreciated, the Bridge should be experienced on foot. Stand in the middle, 135 feet above the East River, look toward Brooklyn, and you will understand viscerally what Hart Crane meant by the structure's "inviolate curve" in *To Brooklyn Bridge*. Any number of

walking tours will present the Bridge's many features and legends: It's the world's first steel-cabled suspension bridge; the designer, John Roebling, was one of twenty-one people who died during its construction; his daughter-in-law, who supervised the Bridge's construction after her husband's health was ruined by "caisson disease" (today it's called the bends), got her law degree at age fifty-five.

Once, if only once, cross the Bridge on foot, alone. The views are breathtaking. The wind whistles, the traffic screams below you, and chill gusts blow off the river. Gaze up at the filigree of spun cable, all 350,000 miles of it. Jump up and down. Nothing to worry about; the Roeblings père and fils designed the Bridge six times stronger than it needed to be. The walk across takes less than half an hour and you'll know why Walt Whitman called the view "the best, most effective medicine my soul has yet partaken."

★ **The Anchorage,** an immensely tall, vaulted space, contains the counterweight for the Brooklyn side of the bridge. It weighs 120,000,000 pounds. To see inside, you'll have to go to a performance there (see p. 53).
★ You can get a glimpse of the BB any time at all on the Internet, via the **Brooklyn Bridge Live Camera** at http://www.romdog.com/bridge/brooklyn.html

To get to the Bridge, take the 4, 5, or 6 trains to Brooklyn Bridge-City Hall (Manhattan side) or the A or C to High Street, Brooklyn (Brooklyn side). If you're walking, the Manhattan entrance is across from City Hall just above Park Row.

"To the Tune of Flutes":
BARGEMUSIC

The *AIA Guide to New York City* affectionately calls it "a floating lump of nonarchitecture." Everyone else calls it **Bargemusic**, Olga Bloom's gift to New York City. In operation for twenty-one years, this former coffee barge is one of the city's foremost performance spaces. Every Thursday evening and Sunday afternoon (more often in summer), people flock down Old Fulton Street to the Fulton Landing where the little barge is berthed. Once inside the cherry-paneled space, they sit, swaying a little with the waves as they listen to chamber music played by the country's best musicians.

Bloom came to the city from Boston in the 1940s to work as a professional violinist; she became one of the first female pit musicians on Broadway. After her retirement, she set up the barge as a relaxed environment where musicians would feel comfortable playing. She makes the audiences just as welcome—with a fireplace, wine and cookies, and her own smiling presence. Bargemusic is small (room for only 130) and has many passionate fans; book well ahead of time.

"In Brooklyn there are so many trees," Bloom said in an interview. "There's care here to make the architecture more varied, not just blocks of the same thing that have no human spirit. That is, of course, what we do in music—we express the human spirit." After a concert is the perfect time to read the stirring Walt Whitman lines engraved on the Fulton Landing railings. Look at the water and think about all the artists, from Whitman to Marianne Moore to Spike Lee, that leafy Brooklyn has nurtured and inspired.

★ And speaking of **Walt Whitman**, his presence is all over this part of Brooklyn. He grew up around the Navy Yard and loved the rowdy, raunchy, and now vanished waterfront. He lived in the borough for close to thirty years. His ghost remains, in the lines of "Crossing Brooklyn Ferry," and also in **Fort Greene Park** (see p. 113) and two buildings— **64 Poplar Street**, in Brooklyn Heights, which Walt and his father allegedly built, and **99 Ryerson Street**, where Whitman lived at the time he completed *Leaves of Grass*. (Paul Berman, a *New Yorker* writer, deduced this through independent research, so don't expect to see a plaque.)

★ For a light supper, try the new **Fulton Ferry Cafe** at the Landing. There are tables inside the renovated Fireboat House and outside on the Landing itself, weather permitting. What a great place to sip a cocktail or eat a sandwich! Call 718-246-3963.

Bargemusic
Fulton Ferry Landing
718-624-4061
Subway: 2 or 3 to Clark Street;
A or C to High Street

Brooklyn Holds Its Liquor:
BARS

Inns, taverns, saloons, gin mills, lounges, taprooms, cantinas, rathskellers, pubs: There are more places to get a drink in Brooklyn than you could possibly visit in a lifetime. Get started with these:

Montero's Bar and Grill, Brooklyn Heights

Don't let the name fool you; there's no grill in here. This is Brooklyn's last waterfront bar (except for the Red Hook Yacht and Kayak Club, see p. 124), even if you do have to cross the Brooklyn-Queens Expressway to get to the waterfront. The cage in the window used to be home to a large parrot. Now it's a parrot memorial. The walls are encrusted with newspaper articles, photos, elaborate model ships, ship's bells and, over the bar, a Montero's sign made of butterfly wings. The mood is gentle and friendly. The only drawback: fifty-odd years of smokers have left an unconquerable tang in the air.

3 Atlantic Avenue 718-624-9799
Subway: 2, 3, 4, 5, to Borough Hall

P. J. Hanley's, Carroll Gardens

This gorgeous place, with its ornate bar, tiled floor, and plentiful plants, claims to be the oldest bar in Brooklyn (1874). It's much more relaxed than its grand setting would suggest. You're as likely to be quaffing alongside a plumber who grew up in the nabe as a recently arrived bond trader. The kitchen sends out unfancy but tasty food. The TVs get good reception and are usually tuned to essential sports events.

449 Court Street 718-834-8223

Subway: F to Carroll Street

Ruby's Old Thyme Bar, Coney Island

Ruby's is sort of a reliquary with a liquor license. Everything in it—including most of the clientele—harks back to Coney's glory days. Only open during the summer months, it's a wonderful place to relax and watch the world, or at least a very funky segment of it, go by in swimsuits.

1213 Boardwalk by W. 12th Street No phone

Subway: B, D, F to Coney Island/
Stillwell Avenue

Teddy's Bar, Williamsburg

Teddy's is a newly hip, but actually quite old, Williamsburg establishment. Fortunately, it's not so hip that a visitor will feel unwelcome. It has all the old bar stuff that's rare in Manhattan but par for the course on our side of the river: mahogany bar (which tilts a bit, spilling your cocktail), tile floor, handsome stained-glass inserts in the front windows. The martinis are good, and so is the bar food—hamburgers, ribs, etc. There's an affable buzz in the place till the wee hours. Weather permitting, they  open the big front windows and let the breeze in. Aaaaaah.

96 Berry Street 718-384-9787

Subway: L to Bedford Avenue

Oh Little Town of
BENSONHURST!

For size, number, and sheer wattage, no neighborhood in all of New York competes with Bensonhurst at Christmastime. The residents of this comfortable, heavily Italian community (with recent infusions of Russians) like their festivals festive. During the Feast of Santa Rosalia (the patron saint of Sicily), for instance, in late August and early September, 15,000 visitors flock to 18th Avenue, Bensonhurst's main street.

The many palatial homes of Bensonhurst range in style from antebellum Southern to Tudor to Cape Cod. These mansions lead the way in decoration, but they are by no means alone. Come the season to be jolly, Bensonhurst homes both big and small are decked out to beat the band. Yards teem with light-encrusted trees, Nativity scenes, and life-size Santas in sleds with reindeer in full flight; flotillas of exuberant elves and masses of gingerbread men crowd each other right up to the property lines. You can see the most elaborate decorations from 79th to 86th Streets, between 11th and 13th Avenues. The indispensable block is 84th Street between 12th and 13th Avenues, where one home, calling itself "Santa's House" for the season, features busy elves at work, Mrs. Claus in her rocking chair, and a smiling, waving

Winnie-the-Pooh. Across the street is a colonnaded mansion in front of which toy soldiers twelve feet high stride slowly in unison, while around them life-size dancing figures cavort in peasant fustian. Over on 82nd Street, at No. 1054, Santa sits in the picture window, tickling the ivories of a grand piano. At 86th Street and 12th Avenue are more massive wooden soldiers. By the end of your trip, the tree and sprigs of holly in your living room will seem pretty measly.

> *Subway: Although a car is the best way to get around here, you can take the B train to 79th Street or 18th Avenue. It's a long ride, so bring a snack.*

The BLACK CHURCHES OF BROOKLYN: A Visit to Concord Baptist Church of Christ

Bridge Street, Siloam, Bethel Tabernacle—Brooklyn's black churches have long been bastions of social stability, cultural awareness, and political change. Some were stations on the Underground Railroad. Later, their Sunday schools provided general education as well as religious training, and they were in the forefront of the civil rights movement of the 1950s and '60s. Today, they provide all sorts of humanitarian services, from day care to drug counseling. Their mission goes far beyond providing places of worship; they seek to help their congregants make their way in a difficult world. To attend a gospel service at one of these churches is not only to hear great music in the setting for which it's intended, but to witness—and briefly participate in—a community of immense spirituality and dignity.

Concord Baptist Church of Christ was founded in 1847 by six free blacks in the home of a woman named Maria Hampton. It was the first black Baptist church in Brooklyn and, through its long and distinguished history, has become an anchor in Bedford-Stuyvesant. With 12,000 congregants, it's the largest black congregation in the country; its social programs include youth groups, elder care, and prison ministries. But on a Sunday morning, as elegantly dressed parishioners flock into the large sanctuary, it is first and foremost a place of devotion.

From the recitation of the congregation's known sick and shut-ins to the Reverend's request for all to join hands and greet those to left and right, in front and back, everything about the service is inclusive. The singing of the gospel choir, supported by drums, piano, and bass, is wonderfully stirring, but it is only a part of the service, not the center. The music is prayer, not performance, and the congregation's singing is every bit as moving as the choir's. So is the moment when families bring their babies, done up, literally, in their Sunday best, for a blessing and a kiss on the forehead from the Reverend.

Although there is great tenderness here, there is little sentimentality. Expect the sermon to address real issues: survival in the city, drugs, joblessness. This is not a passive congregation, either. The call and response between pulpit and pews is constant and heartfelt.

Above all, this experience must be approached with respect. Dress properly, don't snap pictures, don't gape. When the collection plate comes by, contribute. You will be invited to participate, but never pressured. Visitors are asked to rise to be acknowledged by the congregation, and the sincerity of the welcome is obvious and stirring. There is nothing in-your-face or proselytizing about the welcome the outsider receives. It is simply a matter of grace.

Concord Baptist Church

833 Marcy Avenue 718-622-1818
Subway: A to Nostrand Avenue

★ There is great gospel singing all over Brooklyn. The most celebrated group is the large, multicultural choir of the **Brooklyn Tabernacle**, just on the edge of Park Slope, which has recorded many albums, won two Grammys, and toured everywhere. Visitors are welcome but seating is tight, so you are requested to make reservations in writing, well ahead of time.

Brooklyn Tabernacle

290 Flatbush Avenue Brooklyn, N.Y. 11217
718-783-0942, ext. 120
Subway: D or Q to Seventh Avenue

The Russians Have Come,
The Russians Have Come!:
BRIGHTON BEACH

As Soviet communism collapsed, Brighton Beach capitalism surged. This has been the heart of New York's Russian community since the '70s, when Soviet emigration laws were relaxed. Now business is booming, from markets and nightclubs to the man selling shoes from a tiny alley off Brighton Beach Avenue, or the street trumpeter with prerecorded accompaniment who tends to draw more people than money. A visit here feels like a quick trip to a (very) foreign country.

Cafe Society

Russians love the outdoors, and Brighton Beach's Boardwalk bustles year round, in just about any weather. Men hunch over dominos, strollers promenade, cyclists cruise, old folks sit bundled in their wheelchairs, and screeching gulls wheel overhead. Cafes offer everything from blintzes to sushi, in surroundings both elegant (**Tatiana**) and basic (the **Volna**). Sit outside: the sea air is the freshest you will inhale in Brighton Beach, where smoking is not only permitted, it seems to be regarded as a civic duty.

> **Tatiana Cafe**, *3145 Brighton 4th Street,*
> *718-646-7630*
> **Cafe Restaurant Volna**, *3145 Brighton 4th*
> *Street, 718-332-0341*

Main Drag

You'll hear no English spoken as you explore the shops on Brighton Beach Avenue in the dappled shade under the el. Unless your taste runs to big furs (**Classic Galleria**) or saucy lingerie (**Magic Corsets**), you'll be most enthralled by the food. In every deli and shop, it's abundantly displayed. Fish markets offer plump, whole carp, fresh sturgeon, and mysterious varieties of smoked fish. (Serious bargain: salmon caviar for $16 a pound.) In the **Sea Lane Bakery**, shelves groan under mounds of black loaves, challahs, rugelach, and black-and-white cookies. On the second floor of **M & I**, slabs of gooey cake are set out for sale by the pound. On the first floor, you can buy whole beef tongues and livers. If you walk east of 8th Street, the avenue emerges from under the el. Perhaps that's why the **Golden Key** seems more cheerful than the shops in the shadows, full of customers discussing and advising and tasting with evident enjoyment. The elegant **Odessa** offers fancy prepared foods like duck legs with apples, rabbit stew, coulibiac of salmon, and fried whitebait. We think Odessa should open a branch in our neighborhood.

> **Sea Lane Bakery,** *615 Brighton Beach Avenue, 718-934-8877*
> **M & I International Foods,** *249 Brighton Beach Avenue, 718-615-1011*
> **Golden Key,** *1067 Brighton Beach Avenue*
> **Odessa,** *1113 Brighton Beach Avenue, 718-332-3223*

Before you leave, stop at the great—if unprepossessing—**Mrs. Stahl's Knishery**. We like the mushroom with potato, the spinach, and the sweet potato, but they all have their

fans. This is rib-sticking food, to put it mildly; cocktail-size mini-knishes are available, but that's considered cheating.

> *1001 Brighton Beach Avenue*
> *at Coney Island Avenue, 718-648-0210*

★ Brighton Beach teems with nightclubs which, on the outside, have the look of high-end funeral parlors or KGB headquarters. Inside, they're huge and rowdy. Go in a group and appoint a designated driver (see p. 101).

> *Subway: D, Q trains to Brighton Beach*

★ An anomaly in predominantly Polish Greenpoint, the **Russian Orthodox Cathedral of the Transfiguration** is a jewel of a building. It's small, only seating 250, but its high, onion-domed towers give it majesty. Visit on a Sunday morning for Divine Liturgy; the mix of incense, ancient ritual, and sonorous, full-throated singing will make your hair stand on end.

> **Russian Orthodox Cathedral of the**
> **Transfiguration, Greenpoint**
> *228 North 12th Street*
> *Rectory: 718-387-1064*
> *Church Hall: 718-384-9413*
> *Subway: L to Bedford Avenue*

The Principality of Lichtenstein:
BROOKLYN ACADEMY OF MUSIC

Whenever BAM's Brooklyn detractors get all lathered up about Director Harvey Lichtenstein's latest manifestation of creeping Manhattanism, he confounds them by doing something fabulous. That's the way it's gone for the thirty or so years he's been in charge—and he's still at it.

The Brooklyn Academy of Music began in 1861 in Brooklyn Heights, and moved to its current Fort Greene location in 1907 after a fire. Lichtenstein's arrival in 1967 pulled it out of a slump and over the years, he's set an adventurous course, bringing Robert Wilson, Pina Bausch, Mark Morris, and other avant-garde stalwarts into BAM's stately venues. In the '80s, BAM inaugurated the Next Wave Festival and also took over a dilapidated movie palace nearby, turning it into the merely dilapidated-*looking* Majestic Theatre. Despite these achievements, some Brooklynites still tend to see BAM as catering to Manhattan culture-vultures who take the special bus in, maybe grab a bite at Junior's, and then head for home.

Lichtenstein remains indefatigable in pursuit of his dream to make BAM a cultural focus for its neighborhood. He's involved local kids in afterschool programs, and some time at the end of 1998, he's due to bring in a four-screen cinema and a bookstore. The cinema will show a wide variety of independent films, so, although you won't get *Titanic*, you won't be stuck with a steady diet of Rainer Maria Fassbinder. There's a chic little cafe upstairs at the opera house, catered by Michael Ayoub of the wildly successful Park Slope restaurant Cucina (see p. 59). It's open to the public (non-ticket-holders included) before shows, and during intermission (and it's very popular, so arrive early if you want a seat). There's more: the Academy is planning to turn a nearby building into a headquarters for the Mark Morris Company. With all this action, BAM could become a hangout, something the area desperately needs.

Typically, just as Lichtenstein finally gets kudos for attending to his neighbors, he brings in one of the most elite attractions of all—Britain's Royal Shakespeare Company, performing Beckett and the Bard!

★ Pre-show, beat the crush at Junior's and go to the newly opened **New City Bar and Grill** (see p. 61) or **Cambodian Cuisine**, 87 S. Elliott Place (858-3262), the only Cambodian restaurant in New York. This cuisine involves the ingredients you'd expect—coconut, curry, lemongrass, chilis—but it's not as fiery as Thai food, nor as genteel as Vietnamese. Of course you can burn your guts out here should you choose, but you might prefer the Chicken Ahmok, a chicken breast poached in seasoned broth until it achieves an almost puddinglike texture. The many noodle dishes are great.

The Flowers That Bloom in the Spring:
BROOKLYN BOTANIC GARDEN

Give yourself time for the **Brooklyn Botanic Garden**. You'll need it to stroll, sit a while, peer at some leaf or bud, then stroll some more. The grass is great for walking and lying on, since the rules permit no pets and no picnicking (except on special occasions, and only in the Cherry Blossom Esplanade).

It can be crowded—in May, for example, when the cherry trees are in full bloom, and Asian families from all over the city come by in their formal clothes. Or in June, when the Cranford Rose Garden is at its best. Giddy with the fragrance and the glorious color, people mill around in a state of bliss, just-marrieds pose for pictures, and serious rose fanciers try to get a word with Stephen Scanniello, the celebrated rose-man-in-residence.

At most other times, particularly during the week, you'll have this haven pretty much to yourself. In winter, stroll among the bare trees and try to identify them from their skeletal shapes. Warm up in the glasshouses of the Steinhart Pavilion: four temperature-controlled environments, each representing a different climate. Also indoors is the bonsai collection, which will make your jaw drop—but remember, *don't buy one* unless you are prepared to devote your life to the well-being of such a notoriously sensitive creature. In  spring, look for voluptuous magnolias and the crabapples' tangle of sweet-smelling blossoms and graceful limbs. In fall, walk around the pond by the Japanese Garden, with its little Shinto temple and wooden arch. The maples will be ablaze and, if it's a sunny day, the innumerable turtles that live in the pond will have clambered up the rocks for a bask. Keep an eye out for Godzilla, the ancient turtle so monstrously huge (his shell is three feet long) that the tinies cry out when he looms up from the depths.

Special days at the Garden include the **Sakura Matsuri Cherry Blossom Festival** in May, when Japanese singers, dancers, and martial artists perform; the **Chili Pepper Festival** in October, when spicy foods of many lands can be had and everything on sale has a pepper on it; the May **Spring Plant Sale**, when only the strongest survive the stampede to get the best hellebore.

★ You can get acceptable sandwiches and such here, but it's much more fun to go to **Tom's Restaurant** (see p. 129).

(see p. 129)

Brooklyn Botanic Garden
1000 Washington Avenue, 718-622-4433
Subway: 2 or 3 to Eastern Parkway

Note: In the summer, a free shuttle bus runs between the garden and the other cultural institutions in the neighborhood (see p. 142).

(see p. 142).

BROOKLYN CELEBRATES
BIG-TIME: *You Gotta Have . . . Welcome Back . . . Celebrate . . . Atlantic Antic . . . aargh! (A User's Guide) :*

The summer comes, and before you've had time to prepare yourself, it's nonstop Big Bash season. For those who cannot distinguish between the extravaganzas, here's the word:

First, there's **You Gotta Have Park**: Prospect Park-related jollity in the park in mid-May, all proceeds to the park; worthy cause; wholesome fun. The **Welcome Back to Brooklyn Homecoming Festival** takes place in June. It's free, takes place all day around Grand Army Plaza, the library, and the museum and celebrates the borough. Two celebrities are crowned King and Queen and the whole event positively brims with civic pride. Good food, too. **Celebrate Brooklyn** is a wonderfully hip performing-arts festival that runs from the end of June through August at the Prospect Park Bandshell (at 9th Street). In 1998, the festival marked its twentieth season with a spectacular facelift for the bandshell and a greatly expanded lineup, to include silent movies (with live accompaniment), Twyla Tharp, and a performance by monologist Eric Bogosian. But audiences really come to life for the ethnic music performances, from klezmer to reggae. Held in late September, the **Atlantic Antic** is like the Ninth Avenue Food Fair in Manhattan, except that the food is less interesting. In other words, it's a gigantic block party, with performers, merchants selling stained glass, pottery and tie-dye, and other people sitting at tables, trying to get you to join their organizations. Do not take the kids, they'll hate it!

> **You Gotta Have Park,** *718-965-8999*
> **Welcome Back to Brooklyn,** *718-855-7882*
> **Celebrate Brooklyn,** *718-855-7882*
> **Atlantic Antic,** *718-875-8993*

The Giglio, Williamsburg

In June, Williamsburg's Roman Catholics celebrate the feast of St. Paulinus by carrying an enormous, brightly decorated tower of papier-mâché affixed to an aluminum frame through the streets. It weighs about three tons and requires around 125 men to lift and "dance" it—that is, move it through an elaborate series of hoists and pivots. As the procession moves through the streets, thousands of raucous celebrants join it, participating in a neighborhood tradition that began here in 1903. Call 718-384-0223

West Indian Day Parade, Crown Heights

On Labor Day, Eastern Parkway is jammed with hundreds of thousands of West Indian New Yorkers celebrating the last holiday of summer. Down this tree-

lined thoroughfare, an 1870 masterpiece by Frederic Law Olmsted and Calvert Vaux (and the country's first landmarked parkway), enormous floats glide in caravan with rickety trucks carrying steel-drum bands and dancing throngs in gaudy costumes made of feathers, sequins, and not much else. Along the route, you can get some of the best street food to be found in the city: calaloo, rotis, jerk chicken cooked over grills made of halved oil cans. And at 788 Eastern Parkway, Lubavitch World Headquarters, black-clad and bearded Hasidim go about their business as if nothing extraordinary were passing by. But look carefully and you'll see some of their kids jigging to the rhythms of the steel drums. Call 718-625-1515.

BROOKLYN
CELEBRATES LOCALLY:

Let Us Count the Ways:

From the opening of the Little League to St. Patrick's Day, Brooklynites seize any opportunity to get festive (in the case of St. Patrick's Day, on three different days in three different neighborhoods). Here are some of our odder revels:

Blessing of the Fleet, Sheepshead Bay

This forty-four-year-old tradition persists, even though the Sheepshead Bay fleet these days has as many hobbyists and civilians as professional fishermen. Amateurs and pros alike all come together in May for an afternoon of festivities after the boats return from the sea. A pastor, usually someone from the Danish Seamen's Church, will bless the boats, and then people turn to carousing, with music, entertainment, fun for the kids, and general small-town carryings on.

Bay Improvement Group, *718-646-9206*

Blow off the Old, Blow in the New:
New Year's Eve Whistle Blow at Pratt Institute

Since 1965, the Pratt Institute Power House has been the scene of Brooklyn's most unusual New Year's celebration. Chief Engineer Conrad Milster, whose devotion to Pratt's landmark engines is legendary (see p. 111), attaches his collection of antique steam whistles to the generators and runs a pipe outside the building to which students, alums, and visiting enthusiasts can attach their own. Everybody sips champagne and strolls the immaculate Power House gallery, admiring the engines; some wear Victorian garb. Then, on the stroke of midnight, 120 pounds of pressure is released into the line; the whistles uncork their mighty blasts. It's a rowdy, vaporous scene, but much more decorous than Times Square.

This event takes place in front of East Hall on the main Pratt Campus, between Willoughby Street and DeKalb Avenue.

Mermaid Day Parade, Coney Island

For sheer weirdness, this one is hard to beat. It's the brainchild of Dick Zigun, whose arty freak show, Sideshows by the Seashore, is the only live entertainment Coney Island has these days. The Parade happens the first Saturday after the summer solstice, and it celebrates the odd, the antic, and the outrageous with rowdy behavior and many topless participants. The elaborate costumes and floats are homemade; there are lots of prizes. Some Sideshow denizens are involved, so you're likely to see fire-eaters, stilt-walkers, contortionists, and if you're lucky, a marching band called the Vacky Vorld of Vikings.

Coney Island USA, *718-372-5159*

Norwegian-American
Seventeenth of May Parade, Bay Ridge

Brooklyn's once considerable Scandinavian population has dwindled, but one Sunday in May, between confirmation and Mother's Day, Scandinavians from three states descend on Bay Ridge for the Norwegian-American Seventeenth of May Parade. Many of them wear ethnic costumes; there are floats commemorating Nordic heroism in World War II as well as the usual hefty Hibernians playing bagpipes, and assorted vintage cars, policemen, and firefighters. For the big finish, they crown Miss Norway. (How come not in Oslo?)

Call Gail Peterson, 718-851-4678

Polar Bears, Coney Island

For some people, many of them Russian, the perfect

way to celebrate New Year's Day is by plunging into the frigid waters off Coney Island. Three hundred or so hardy souls, many of whom have stayed up all night, start with calisthenics on the sand around 1:00 P.M., then swim. Anyone who goes in gets a certificate. The Atlantis Bar on the Boardwalk will be open for swimmers and gawkers alike.

Coney Island USA, *718-372-5159*

Watching the July 4th Fireworks in Greenpoint

This old-fashioned Polish enclave contains a key Brooklyn insider site—the best place to watch the July 4th fireworks over the East River. Take the G train to Greenpoint Avenue and walk to West Street. Turn right, and walk three blocks to India Street. Turn left. This pier will give you a breathtaking view of the fireworks, and you'll be surrounded by hundreds of happy immigrants in their lawn chairs, watching the show and listening to the music on the radio.

Walking through History:
BROOKLYN HEIGHTS

This neighborhood is unique in New York City. It has survived intact and remains today almost exactly as it was built—six hundred or so houses here predate the Civil War. Walk uphill, from south to north, and you go back in time—from the solid, suburban splendor of the late nineteenth century back to more ramshackle days, when the real action was down on the waterfront, in a rowdy, thriving village that grew up around the ferry landing. Why not take a leisurely walking tour, using Hope Cooke's *Seeing New York* and the *AIA Guide to New York City*? Be sure not to miss the following gems.

Garden Place, between Joralemon and State Streets, is today's most desirable Heights block—gorgeous, secluded, and requiring buckets of money to live there. **Willow Place's** colonnaded homes are more than 150 years old, the last of their kind in Brooklyn. **Grace Court** is a sweet alley leading to Grace Church (see p. 128), designed in 1847 by Richard Upjohn. (Gaze up at the grand old elm tree before going inside.) Built by Frank Freeman in 1890, the **Herman Behr House** at No. 84 Pierrepont is a full-blown beauty which has been, variously, a hotel, the headquarters of Xaviera Hollander and her lovelies, and a Franciscan residence. Now, it's a condo.

Stroll north on **Willow Street** and notice how the scale changes, mansions giving way to smaller, often wood-framed houses, built and owned by the artisans and tradespeople working at the waterfront. The lovely red Federal houses at 155, 157, and 159 Willow date back to 1829; 151 was allegedly a link in the Underground Railroad (the glass bricks in the sidewalk said to be there to light the tunnel for runaway slaves). There's an unexpected redwood at 155. Architecture enthusiasts will recognize the Shingle style of Richard Norman Shaw at 108, 110, 112 (1880).

Plymouth Church of the Pilgrims, on Orange Street, was built in 1849 for the celebrated (and notorious) abolitionist preacher, Henry Ward Beecher. Lincoln worshiped here, and Beecher held mock slave auctions at the altar (and it has Tiffany windows, see p. 128). On one of the oldest streets in the neighborhood, you'll find its prettiest house. **Middagh Street** dates from 1817, and No. 24, a dormered Federal house built in 1824, has a gorgeous doorway, leaded glass panes, and a little cottage in its garden.

You're close to the water here. To get that orientation, go north on **Hicks Street** and check out the pretty houses numbered 38, 38A, and 40. Look up the alley leading to 38A and you'll see the original fronts of the houses. Dating from the 1790s, they looked out over the bustle of the ferry landing. In the 1840s, when gentrification struck, the houses literally turned away from the water.

Subway: 2, 3, 4, 5 to Borough Hall

For Art's Sake:
BROOKLYN MUSEUM OF ART

This is an old-fashioned temple of culture, and it looks the part. A huge, Beaux Arts pile, it contains the nation's second-largest collection of art. Between the breadth of its holdings and the occasional big-ticket exhibit that trundles through (the Monet, the

Romanov Jewels), only 6 percent of its collection can be displayed at any time. Still, you can sample the entire spectrum of the visual arts in this one place—and in peace and quiet, since the Brooklyn aspect tends to deter the tourists and the ladies-who-

lunch. This is a never-ending frustration for the museum's officials. For you, it's a pleasure.

Sure, they have Rodin and Degas, Cézanne and Matisse, but for your first visit, why not start with *our* favorites?

Fifth floor: O'Keeffe's *Brooklyn Bridge* makes you realize the power of an original over its reproductions. The euphoric landscapes of Hudson River School artists Thomas Cole and Frederic Church depict dreams of the New World, while Francis Guy's *Winter Scene in Brooklyn* (1820), in which every person is modeled from life, seems as reliable a record as a photo. One of the two Gilbert Stuart portraits of Washington depicts a much younger man than you're used to seeing. The Lachaise nude is breathtaking (giggle-inducing if you're under ten).

Fourth floor: Behold the gorgeous stained-glass panel by Walter Cole Brigham, into which shells, stones, and thick sea glass are incorporated. Also check out the Fantasy Furniture collection, including a wooden dragon chair and a garden set modeled on peacock feathers. Why can't they make modern vacuum cleaners as pretty as the Electrolux in the Design collection? Best of all are the twenty-eight period rooms, some of them flanked by tiny, atmospheric models of the houses they came from. Too bad you can't move into the honey-colored Art Deco study (complete with a walk-in bar that was hidden behind paneling during Prohibition). Don't miss the Victorian parlor, with its mysterious child mannequin turned tantalizingly away from you as she plays with her Noah's Ark and winding column of wooden animals.

Third floor: The superb Egyptian collection contains faience animals and erotic ceramics (honest!), and also a real, honest-to-goodness, dimly lit, spooky-for-the-kids mummy.

Second floor: The carpets in the Islamic and Oriental collections really do look magical.

First floor: *Primitive* seems an inappropriate description for these haunting pieces from Africa, the Americas, and the Pacific, but that's what they call 'em. There are totem poles, Native American clothes with intricate designs, and the exquisite, 2,000-year-old Paracas Textile from Peru. The stately entrance hall usually houses some specially commissioned modern extravaganza. The cafe serves forgettable food (remember, the divine Tom's is just blocks away, see p. 129), but the gift shop is one of the best of its kind. Along with the usual arty neckties and posters, you'll find interesting books, jewelry from around the world, and an array of artisanal garments and objects (not to mention a bright red Waring blender).

The Brooklyn Museum of Art's original mission

was the "education, refinement, elevation, and pleasure of all the people." As you leave, weary and exhilarated, you'll feel that the mission has been accomplished, without a doubt.

★ On the first Saturday of the month the Museum is open
til 11 PM, with free admission and parking after 6 PM, and
live dance music in the Great Hall starting at 9 PM. Talk
about somethiing for everyone!

Brooklyn Museum of Art
200 Eastern Parkway, 718-638-5000
Subway: 2, 3 to Eastern Parkway/
Brooklyn Museum of Art

Down to the Sea in Ships:
BROOKLYN NAVY YARD

During the Second World War, 70,000 men and women
worked round-the-clock shifts at the Brooklyn Navy
Yard, where the motto was "Can do." The *Arizona*,
sunk at Pearl Harbor, was built here; so was the
Missouri, on board which the Japanese surrendered;
so was Robert Fulton's steamboat, the *Clermont*, and
so was the *Maine*. Remember the *Maine*? Shipbuilding
began here in 1799 and continued until 1965. But the
Navy Yard today is no shrine, it's a thriving industrial
park—and the most important historic site in New
York City that is (mostly) closed to the general public.

The Yard's jumble of buildings (the Victorian pay-
master's house, a World-War-II-era Quonset hut) is

occupied by manufacturers of furniture, modular housing, Sweet'n Low, and scenery for soap operas. Fireboats, Staten Island ferries, and Circle Line vessels are repaired here. There's a building where cash boxes are filled with cash and another from which ground shark's fins and sea horses are exported. And soon, the Navy Yard will contain the nation's largest film and television production studio, comprising fifteen acres and eleven sound stages.

Amid the bustle, remnants—sometimes very large remnants—of the past remain. Take Dry Dock #1, for instance. The smallest of the four operational dry docks at the Yard, it was built in 1851; within its smooth, granite walls the Civil War ironclad *Monitor* was outfitted for combat! And then there's the sign over a dark entrance to Building 292, indicating a fourth-floor cafeteria that hasn't existed since the '40s.

Most of the historic buildings are still in government hands and strictly off-limits to civilians, though the **Commandant's House**, completed in 1806 and thought to be the finest Federal house in Brooklyn, is in use as a conference center. Glimpse it over the wall at the corner of Little and Evans Streets. Between Ryerson Street and Williamsburg Place stands the landmark **Naval Hospital**, made of marble quarried by inmates at Sing Sing; legend has it that some of the Prison Ship Martyrs memorialized in Fort Greene Park are buried

nearby. Most interesting and mysterious are the ten houses of **Admiral's Row**, mansions built for officers in the 1820s and '30s. Uninhabited and unprotected for thirty years, they may not be around much longer. You can still see these majestic buildings, though, if the trees are not in leaf, through the tops of the chicken-wire fencing on Flushing Avenue and Navy Street, across from Commodore Barry Park.

Occasionally you can get into the Navy Yard itself; keep an eye out for the annual tour offered by the 92nd Street Y. Besides its wonderful views of the bridges and the river, the Yard has a tangible spirit. You can even feel it on the Brooklyn-Queens Expressway. Next time you're stuck in traffic between the Flushing and Kent/Wythe exits, look off toward Manhattan. That big ghostly building on the knoll is the Naval Hospital.

★ Right outside the Navy Yard's gates is **Reliable & Franks Naval Uniforms**, a genuine military surplus store, established in 1927. They sell no copies, no fakes; the merchandise is strictly the real deal. Troll the crowded, dusty aisles for pea jackets and all manner of military hats at prices that are as antediluvian as the place itself.

Brooklyn Navy Yard
Flushing Avenue to the East River, Hudson and Navy Streets to Kent Avenue, 718-852-1441
Reliable & Franks Naval Uniforms
106 Flushing Avenue, 718-858-6033
Subway: F to York Street

Moonstruck Brooklyn:

CARROLL GARDENS

South of the Heights and Cobble Hill lies the old Italian neighborhood of Carroll Gardens, long said to be one of the city's safest because the parents of so many "made men" lived here. Even though outsiders have begun to move in, Carroll Gardens remains, essentially, an old Italian neighborhood.

Around the turn of the century, immigrants began arriving from Bari, on the Adriatic, and most settled close to the Red Hook waterfront, where they worked. The residents of Carroll Gardens are their descendants, which explains why there is a statue of Maria SS Adolorato Patrona di Mola di Bari in the garden of a social club on the corner of Court and Fourth Streets.

The immigrants came to a highly distinctive place. The oldest part of Carroll Gardens, 1st through 4th Places between Henry and Smith Streets, was laid out in 1846 in "deep blocks," giving the houses both front and back gardens. This plan was maintained as the neighborhood expanded. The result is street after street of vernal beauty, with row houses set back from the street behind lush gardens, and narrow sidewalks canopied by foliage. The gardens are impeccable, and many contain painted Madonnas or St. Francis bird-baths, plaster deer or sheep. At Christmas the displays rival Bensonhurst's (p. 18) in enthusiasm, if not size.

There are some unusual houses here, like the row at numbers 3–7a on 2nd Place between Court and Henry Streets, with wooden overhangs protecting their front doors and mansarded roof lines. Continuity and change coexist peacefully. The former Westminster Presbyterian Church on the corner of 1st Place and Clinton Street is one of several big old churches around here that have been converted to condos. Next door is one of the most beautiful Greek Revival buildings in New York. The **John Rankin residence** is a foursquare red-brick building from 1840, with full-height pilasters at the corners and a majestic doorway, and it's scrupulously maintained by its current occupant, the Guido Funeral Home.

Walking on these streets, you are struck by the quiet. When it's warm, old folks sit on folding chairs in their gardens, and children play games on streets that see little traffic. Shopping here feels like a trip to another time. At **Dave's 5 & 10**, a genuine notions shop, you can find window-shade pulls, flowerpots, string, trash cans, Barbie dolls, ice-cube trays, champagne glasses, coloring books, and stovetop espresso makers in the full range of sizes, all on one creaky, wooden sales floor. In **Caputo's**, a hole-in-the-wall appetizing store, a woman who speaks no English sells ciabatta, focaccia, beautiful fresh mozzarella, and the harder to find scamorza (dried mozzarella). Have lunch farther up Court Street at **Helen's Place**, an old-fashioned red-Italian restaurant with white tablecloths and a linoleum floor, wood-paneled walls, and a Golden-Age-of-Radio atmosphere. Stop for coffee at **Sinatra's Museum Caffe Nostalgia and Coo Coo Nest**, a second-floor coffee bar that is also a memorabilia-encrusted shrine to the Kid from

Hoboken. Buy some beans to take home from **D'Amico Foods**, where they've been roasting them for fifty years. Finally, head over to Henry and Sackett Streets. Next door to the

Little Chatterbox Beauty Salon was the late, lamented Cammareri Brothers Bakery, where Cher's suitor worked in *Moonstruck*. But at **Monteleone's**, back on Court, they still make Italian pastries the old-fashioned way, and their delicate lemon ice actually tastes like lemon!

Rankin Residence, *440 Court Street*
Dave's 5 & 10, *439 Court Street,*
718-875-2517
Caputo's, *460 Court Street,*
718-855-8852
**Sinatra's Museum Caffe Nostalgia
and Coo Coo Nest**, *371 Court Street,*
718-855-0587
Helen's Place, *396 Court Street,*
718-855-9128
D'Amico Foods, *309 Court Street,*
718-875-5403
Frank Monteleone's Pastry Shop, *355 Court
Street, 718-624-9253*
Subway: F or G to Carroll Street

Yes, It Can Be Done!
CLOTHES SHOPPING
in Brooklyn

You can find discount designer clothing at **Century 21** in Bay Ridge, **Loehmann's** in Sheepshead Bay, and **S&W** in Flatbush—but the following are more elementally Brooklyn in nature:

Kleinfelds in Bay Ridge is "the largest bridal house in the world" and mecca for a million trembling brides. Whether or not you actually plan to buy The Gown here, a trip to check it out is as essential as the announcement. The Kleinfelds experience is not exactly restful, but the selection is enormous and varied—not just heaps of tulle and organdy—and the prices are right, from $1,200 to over $10,000. Before you go, book an appointment, and form a clear idea of what you're after (preferably illustrated with pictures) and what you're prepared to pay. Cultivate nerves of steel, the better to ignore the maelstrom of tension churning all around and to cope with your relentless "personal consultant."

8206 5th Avenue, 718-833-1100
Subway: R to 86th Street

Domsey's Warehouse Outlet in Williamsburg is where the groovy and deeply strapped go to pore over surplus restaurant uniforms, secondhand baseball jackets, and cocktail gowns. For just a few bucks, you can come out of there with a grunge/art student/retro look that equips you perfectly for life in Williamsburg or the

East Village. The best bargains here are in the surplus/ closeout sections (tons of Army and fire department stuff), or upstairs in vintage clothes, where, bearing labels like  "International Scene," there are velour jackets from $5–$7, evening dresses for under $10, and leather coats for under $20. There are fitting rooms on the premises. And if you're of a mind to stock up on garden hoses, kitchen gadgets, or other inexpensive household items, you'll be one happy shopper.

431 Kent Avenue, 718-384-6000
Subway: J or M to Marcy Avenue

Women from Brownstone Brooklyn go to **Tango** in Brooklyn Heights to browse amid quietly tasteful clothes while thanking their lucky stars they don't have to shlep around Manhattan. In business for twenty years, Tango knows its customers and offers them a good range of bridge and "contemporary sportswear," featuring lines such as Max Mara and Tahari. What's nice here is the individual attention and the fact that they stock really good shoes (Cole-Haan, Charles Jourdan) and accessories.

145 Montague Street, 718-625-7518
Subway: 2, 3, 4, 5, to Borough Hall

CONEY ISLAND
of the Mind

Coney is a place for all seasons and moods. Walk, freezing, along the beach in winter, when there's snow on the sand, Russians in furs out for a stroll, and the gulls wheeling and screeching all around you. Go on a scorching weekend in August when many thousands of people converge to make a temporary home for themselves and their beach towels. Whenever you go, Coney will give you a thrill.

What's still there? There's the decrepit elevated subway station at Coney Island/Stillwell Avenue—only in Brooklyn can you take the subway to the sea! At the bottom of the steps, as you emerge onto Surf Avenue, there's **Philip's Candy Store**, where a kind and courtly man named John Dorman has been making and selling traditional candy—chocolate-covered bananas, taffy apples, and peanut brittle—for over forty years.

Now cross the street and rush past the rowdy attractions to the Boardwalk, spine of the Nickel Empire, and beyond it, the wide beach and the sea. Off to the left, there's a breakwater that roughly divides Coney Island from Brighton Beach, and on those rocks are carved about a dozen mythical-looking faces, chiseled by some unremembered artist. A few years ago, the U.S. Army Corps of Engineers buried them all under four feet of sand as part of a beach renovation project. One has now reemerged; the others will be along shortly, tides permitting.

The stouthearted will want to ride the legendary

Cyclone (all eighty-five feet, nine hills, 60 mph, and 100 seconds of it) or the **Tiltawhirl**, a ride so nauseating that only children can stand it. Visit the tiny **Coney Island USA**

museum, or buy a ticket to **Sideshows by the Seashore**, where you'll see snake-charmers, fire-eaters, escape artists, and interestingly pierced and tattooed people doing their odd things. Here, and at the year-round **Faber's Arcade**, where you can play skee-ball and shoot'em up games, you'll see languid hipsters in black, local teens, and families from all over, all with the benign, befuddled air that overtakes people when they're here.

For some glimpses of Coney's innocently seedy past, wander by the dilapidated **Thunderbolt** roller coaster (recently fire-damaged) and the rusted **Parachute Jump** (a relic of the 1939 World's Fair). Check out **Ruby's Old Thyme Bar** on the Boardwalk (see p. 17), or go back across Surf Avenue to the **B&B Carousell** [sic], which has survived for sixty years under the el, with its carnival music, horses and chariots—and real brass rings for you to catch. There's a deeply weird Russian flea market all around it. And finally, before you go home, follow your nose to **Nathan's** (see p. 59).

Philip's Candy Store, *1237 Surf Avenue, 718-372-8783*

Sideshows by the Seashore/Coney Island USA, *1208 Surf Avenue, 718-372-5101/5159*
Faber's Arcade, *3017 Stillwell Avenue, 718-265-4972*
Nathan's Famous Restaurant, *1310 Surf Avenue near Stillwell Avenue, 718-946-2202 Subway: B, D, F, N to Coney Island/ Stillwell Avenue*

Busy Hands:
CRAFTS SHOPS
and Studios

To many people, the word *craft* conjures up an image of earnest artisans and dingy pottery. These places will make you reexamine your prejudices and take out your wallet.

Breukelen (and Bark)

Atlantic Avenue antiques browsers are pleasantly surprised when they enter this store—pair of stores, actually—with the old-fashioned name and the *au courant* inventory. Breukelen, in front, sells everything from vases to candles to decidedly offbeat kitchen appliances. In back, Bark specializes in quality textiles—kimonos, Egyptian cotton blankets. Both sell unusual furniture pieces. You'll find yourself eyeing things you never knew you wanted—an elegant lamp made from an air filter, say. Air filter?

    Breukelen, *718-246-0024*

Bark, *718-625-8997*

369 Atlantic Avenue, bet. Hoyt and Bond Streets

Subway: 2 or 3 to Hoyt Street; F to Bergen Street

The Clay Pot

This is a rarity—a Brooklyn store known outside Brooklyn! More than 3,000 couples a year come to the Clay Pot in Park Slope for engage-ment or wedding rings and find what they're after—something handcrafted, beautiful, and differ-ent. The Clay Pot has prospered in a brutal climate for small busi-ness because its wares are so wisely and tastefully chosen. Besides the tempting scarves, ceramic and wooden pieces,

there's enough interesting jewelry to create indecision in the most hard-nosed shopper. The staff is very patient. Warning: On spring weekends, you'll have to fight your way through hordes of dewy-eyed couples taking their time.

162 7th Avenue, Park Slope, 718-788-6564

Subway: D, Q, to Seventh Avenue;

F to Seventh Avenue

Brooklyn Artisans Gallery

What sets this little Cobble Hill store apart is that it's a cooperative business owned and run by the local artists who create the items on display. Pottery and ceramics predominate, but you can also buy glass, jewelry, fabric items, and so on. The artists them-selves work there, which means that you can talk to them and request custom pieces in a particular color or size. Prices start at $3.50 for handmade paper cards and go up to hundreds for gorgeously hand-painted silk scarves or large mosaic mirrors.

221A Court Street, 718-330-0343

Subway: F to Bergen Street; 2, 3, 4, 5

to Borough Hall

Urban Glass

New York's only art-glass-working center is in a loft above an old theater in downtown Brooklyn. Walk in and you'll feel you're in a medieval inferno. The big space is hot, *seriously* hot, and dominated by three huge furnaces that glow with orange light. Sweaty students hoist globs of molten glass on long rods in and out of them, while neon-benders and glass-bead-mak-ers toil nearby. This is the hub of East Coast glass-blowing, and the country's most renowned glass artists come to exhibit their work or teach classes. To experience the high of glassblowing, take a course. To get the thrill vicariously, stop by for one of the monthly open houses or a performance art event. Don't overlook the good gift shop, where you can buy pieces made on the premises.

57 Rockwell Place, 718-625-3685

Subway: 2, 3, 4, 5 to Nevins Street; D, Q, R, N

to DeKalb Avenue

See It While You Can:
DUMBO

Visiting Dumbo is not at all like visiting Williamsburg. Cafes? Shopping? There are absolutely none, but who cares? Not the residents.

Dumbo (Down Under the Manhattan Bridge Overpass, in case you were wondering) encompasses most of the area between the Brooklyn and Manhattan Bridges. To understand why people are drawn to this remote outpost, stand at the foot of Old Fulton Street, facing the River Cafe and Manhattan. Turn right along Water Street, under the Brooklyn Bridge, then first left, down to the water and the cobblestones surrounding the bridge's great tower. Whatever season, whatever time of day, this waterside view will render you speechless. The big industrial buildings behind you are full of crafts workshops and artists. Look for the grassy Empire–Fulton Ferry State Park (great for a picnic) and, on Water Street, the Empire Stores, a beautiful warehouse built in 1870.

Of course, there's a struggle over this priceless stretch of waterfront. Will it remain a pocket of affordable loft space for artists and small businesses, or will the developers turn it into a giant retail/entertainment mecca like Pier 17 just across the river? See it now, before you need your credit card.

★ Visit during an event, if you want to see the place come to life. **The Anchorage** (see p. 13) is open during the summer for art and music events. Expect the groovy. (Call **Creative Time** at 212-206-6674 or visit the Website, www.creativetime.org, for information.) During **Art Under the Bridge** weekend in October, studios are open, bands play in the street, and there are multimedia installations, deadly serious performance art and (our personal favorite) a public life-class featuring several nude models and dozens of painters in a warm loft space redolent with incense. The good old avant-garde lives! Watch for a listing.

★ **Grimaldi's Pizzeria** at 19 Old Fulton Street (718-858-4300) offers brick-oven-baked pizza so thin-crusted, smoky, and delicious that it satisfies all age groups. There's almost always a line, but it moves fast and once you get inside, Sinatra will probably be playing.

Subway: A to High Street; F to York Street

Dueling
DUTCH HOUSES:
If you can't choose which one to see, see 'em all!

There aren't many traces of the Dutch left in New York City, but Southern Brooklyn has the mother lode: fifteen houses, including the official oldest building in New York State (it's a museum, but most of the others are in private hands). You'll need a car to see them all because they're not clustered, but Gravesend and

Flatlands are easy to navigate, and it's thrilling to spot a Dutch farmhouse, with its sloping ("gambrel") roof, surrounded by the twentieth century. Some construction dates are  approximate, since the documentation is fragmentary.

1. Most haunting: Hendrick I. Lott House, 1940 E. 36th Street, c. 1720 with 1800 addition. Rambling, deserted place with two porches, one with square columns, the other with round. All boarded up, peeling shingles. Big yard, shady and overgrown, and recently the site of an archaeological dig. Owned by the Lott family for almost three hundred years. In May '98, after a concerted effort by neighbors, family, and private organizations, funds were made available for "emergency stabilization." Scheduled to be a museum.

2. Most unrecognizable: Schenck (Stoothoff)-Williamson [sic], 1587 E. 53rd Street, 1797. It has this yellow-brick facade . . .

3. Most seamlessly part of the neighborhood: Johannes Van Nuyse/Coe, 1128 E. 34th Street, 1806. Big roof. White birch tree and dogwood in yard. Cute picket fence (c. 1930, probably). Neighbors include a body shop, used car lots, and a storefront Wesleyan church.

4. Most fragmentary: Ryder–Van Cleef, 38 Village Road, c. 1750? 1840? Who knows? But the fragment is clearly recognizable.

5. Most thoroughly genteel restoration: Pieter

Claesen Wyckoff, 5902 Clarendon, at intersection of Ralph and Ditmas Avenues. Sweet, small, brown-shingled place, claimed to be 1652 with later additions. Sits in sloping meadow in middle of urban tumult. Officially the oldest building in New York State. A museum, with some Wyckoff family items inside. Call 718-629-5400 to visit.

6. Most denigrated: Lady Deborah Moody/ Van Sicklen, 17 Gravesend Neck Road. Late 1600s–early 1700s. Uglied up with lots of fake trim. A Victorian developer claimed it was the home of Lady Deborah Moody, the English Anabaptist who fled persecution and founded Gravesend in 1643. (She's buried in the tiny cemetery opposite, see p. 77). Experts cast doubts, but acknowledge that it's very old.

7. Best value for your old-Dutch-house moment: Wyckoff-Bennett Homestead, 1669 E. 22nd Street. Date "1766" is cut into one of the beams. Clapboard and shingle beauty has deep porch and Dutch doors. Used by Hessians during the Revolutionary War; a couple of them scratched their names into a windowpane.

8. Easiest to find: Jan Martense Schenk, 1676. Moved from Flatlands, immaculately restored and relocated to fourth floor of the Brooklyn Museum of Art (see p. 36).

9. Most pathetic: First Elias Hubbard Ryder, 2138 McDonald Avenue, 1750. Hidden under elevated subway tracks, buried under vegetation, the house is there. But not for long, we suspect.

10. Furthest flung: Bloom-Stoothoff, 494

Jamaica Avenue, c. 1790s. Way up on the Queens border, this big old house survives, but you'll have to look hard to spot it, under all the new siding, new windows, and little turrets.

11. Second most unrecognizable: Van Pelt–Woolsey, 4011 Hubbard Place, 1791. It's newly renovated, on a tiny stretch of old Dutch road.

12. Most imposing: Stoothoff-Baxter-Kouwenhoven, 1640 E. 48th Street, 1747, altered in 1811. Built by Flemish immigrants on four hundred long-gone acres. Handsome, with shutters in good condition and tiny lead-framed upstairs windows. Ancient horse chestnut tree, another cute picket fence out front.

13. Most inappropriate columns: Van Nuyse–Magaw, 1041 E. 22nd Street, 1803. Moved to this spot in 1916 and turned to fit its narrow lot.

14. Most unnecessary gaslights: Second Elias Hubbard Ryder, 1926 E. 28th Street, 1834. The shutters are modern, too.

15. Most kid-friendly: Lefferts Homestead, 1777, in Prospect Park. It's a folk museum and children's activity center (see p. 88).

Brooklyn EATS I:
The Institutions

Brennan and Carr

Sixty years of hot beef sandwiches and burgers at the same address; the fried cheese sticks came later, no doubt. The wood-paneled dining room has wagon-wheel chandeliers and lace curtains. Comfy room, comfy food. The fries are excellent. Soft drinks are served in paper cups.

3432 Nostrand Avenue, Marine Park,
718-382-4500
Subway: D to Avenue U (a long walk from
the station)

Gage and Tollner

The kitchen is capricious at this venerable place, so stick to the classics: she-crab soup, broiled clam bellies, and (if they have it) the stuffed whole Vidalia onion appetizer. Food has never really been as important here as the room itself, long and graceful, with its dark wood paneling, gas lamps, and streaky old mirrors. The waiters receive chevrons for their years of service, and some of them are as decorated as General MacArthur.

372 Fulton Street, Downtown Brooklyn,
718-875-5181
Subway: A, F to Jay Street/Borough Hall

Peter Luger Steakhouse

Don't expect special treatment here. Brusque waiters shuffle around the sawdust-covered floor, deflecting requests for menus with "First tell me how you like your steak done." Well, the steaks really are amazing, and so are the fist-sized lamb chops. Obviously, generations of shirt-sleeved guys sipping Chivas with their T-bones aren't wrong. (Cash or Luger's card only.)

178 Broadway, Williamsburg, 718-387-0500
Subway: J, M to Marcy Avenue

Lundy Brothers

Even at half its former size, it's bigger than any restaurant you've ever seen, but much more inviting than the Moorish mess hall of yore. For one thing, they don't let people waiting for tables loom over seated diners any more. The shore dinner is a ton of food, but who wants half a chicken here? Go for the raw shellfish and simple preparations like steamed or broiled lobster and fried shrimp. The biscuits are to die for. In case you're wondering, the enigmatic initials F.W.I.L. on the waiters' jackets stand for Frederick Irving William Lundy, the restaurant's founder.

1901 Emmons Avenue, Sheepshead Bay
718-743-0022
Subway: D, Q to Sheepshead Bay

Junior's

It's cheerful and open till all hours, and its vast menu offers everything from barbecue to matzoh ball soup. Most of it's just okay, but then there's the cheesecake. It's the essential item on the menu and you'll dream about it for weeks after you've tried it. Fortunately, you can buy one to take home. Ignore the fruit-topped ones and do what the pros do: order the plain.

386 Flatbush Avenue
Downtown Brooklyn,
718-852-5257
Subway: D, M, N, Q,
R to DeKalb Avenue

Monte's Italian Restaurant

Monte's has been dishing up sturdy Neapolitan food at this address since 1906 (with a two-year hiatus in 1992–93). The Venetian murals on the walls have been here for fifty years; so have some of the waiters. Don't be put off by its unromantic location (a stone's throw from the Gowanus Canal); there's valet parking and a warm welcome from a staff that knows what it's doing.

451 Carroll Street, Gowanus, 718-624-8984
Subway: M, N, R to Union Street

Nathan's Famous Restaurant

The annual July 4th hot-dog-eating contest here dates back to 1916, but forget history. And forget Sabrett's, Hebrew National, Papaya King, the Yankee Stadium dogs, even the sainted Leo's of 32nd Street. The original Nathan's serves the best hot dog in New York, which is to say, the universe. Other Nathan's branches do not approach the standards of the mother ship. The fries are sublime too, not to mention the kraut . . . and the mustard. . . .

1310 Surf Avenue, Coney Island, 718-946-2202
Subway: B, D, F, N to Coney Island

Brooklyn EATS II:
Cutting-Edge Cuisine

Cucina

When Michael Ayoub's Italian restaurant opened in 1990, Brooklynites couldn't believe how good it was, especially for a restaurant in Brooklyn. It's still that good, and, consequently, so popular that you'll need a reservation on weekends and some busy weeknights. A particular joy of Cucina has always been the stunning display of antipasti; our favorites include the onion and olive tart and the white beans with little shrimp. Other excellent dishes: the red snapper with clams and any meat dish, particularly the osso bucco. This is a very civilized place: the service is quietly efficient, the tables are large and well spaced—for once, a hot restaurant offers elbow room. The small wine list always includes a number of good selections for around $20. Cucina isn't exactly cheap; entrees run from $15 into the twenties. But given the quality, it's a bargain.

256 Fifth Avenue, Park Slope, 718-230-0711

Subway: M, N, R to Union Street;

2, 3 to Bergen Street

The River Cafe

Tucked away on its little barge right by the Brooklyn Bridge, the River Cafe boasts one of the truly great restaurant views. It's such a romantic setting—and such a shame that most of the people eating there seem to be business types on expense accounts. As for the food, it's the kind of high-concept, high-style cuisine that Brooklynites of not so long ago would have called "fancy-shmancy," and it's just as divine as you'd expect. If you don't want to wait for a special occasion, you could just go for drinks or weekend brunch. Whenever you go, remember to book well in advance.

1 Water Street, Fulton Landing, 718-522-5200
Subway: A or C to High Street

New City Bar and Grill

Rebecca Scanlon and Raoul Richardson opened the New City Cafe, their very first, very elegant restaurant in the garden floor of a Fort Greene brownstone, and made it a hit. Now they've moved, to a location directly across from the Brooklyn Academy of Music. Opening in the fall of 1998, in a former hotel lobby with a gorgeous plaster ceiling, the new restaurant is twice the size of the old. Expect it to be "a little bit looser, more American" than their previous one, say the owners, with a bar menu, pre- and post-theater dinners, and Sunday brunch. The food they serve is nouvelle French-American, prepared with imagination and pizzazz. In short, it's definitely worth sampling.

25 Lafayette Avenue, Fort Greene, 718-622-5607
Subway: 2, 3, 4, 5, B, D, Q to Atlantic Avenue

Max and Moritz

This is a sleeper—an excellent small bistro that's not yet widely known. The people who do know it are crazy about it. Why? Because the space is comfortable and welcoming, and the French-inspired food is beautifully prepared. You may be agreeably surprised by some of the combinations—a corn and goat-cheese tart, say—but you never have the feeling of being subjected to someone's Big Idea. This is fabulous food in a place with a neighborhood feel.

426A Seventh Avenue, Park Slope, 718-499-5557
Subway: F to Seventh Avenue

Brooklyn **EATS III**: Ethnic Food

Sampling every type of ethnic food available in Brooklyn would be a lifetime occupation—and one we'd gladly undertake. Here are some favorites:

Brawta

You can find West Indian patty shops all over Brooklyn (our favorite is **Christie's**, a sliver of a place on the corner of Flatbush Avenue and Sterling Place), but for a sit-down Caribbean meal, try Brawta, an airy cafe in the heart of the Atlantic Avenue antiquing district. There's art on the walls and good music, but the delicately spiced food is the reason to be here: brown stewed chicken, curried goat, escoviche of fish, ital (vegetable) stew, and the Jamaican national dish, akee, served in portions that dare you to finish them. There's no liquor, but the unusual fruit drinks (sorrel, fiery ginger beer), provide a quiet buzz without alcohol.

> *347 Atlantic Avenue*
> *Boerum Hill, 718-855-5515*
> *Subway: A, G to Hoyt-Schermerhorn*

Christie's Jamaican Patties
334 Flatbush Avenue, Park Slope, 718-636-9746
Subway: D or Q to Seventh Avenue

Mabat

Mabat is kosher—there's even a sink in the dining room for the ritual pre-prandial wash. What distinguishes it is the Sephardic-style food, more delicate than the kugel and corned beef usually thought of as the Chosen's cuisine of choice. There are no menus, but everything's on display. The silky eggplant exudes garlic, the chopped Israeli salad has a touch of heat, and the avocado is mashed with hard-boiled egg and scallions. But the grill is the star of the show: the steaks and skewers of sweetbreads, chicken thighs, and lamb are just  superb—juicy, crisp, perfect. Kosher food is never cheap, but it's worth it at this spare storefront.

1809 East 7th Street, Kings Highway,
718-339-3300
Subway: D, F, Q to Kings Highway

The McCafe

(formerly McDonald's Stuyvesant Heights Cafe)
Founded in 1948, this is the oldest black restaurant in Brooklyn, and its menu reflects the diverse tastes of its clientele: shrimp étouffée, jerk chicken, grits, and wraps. But mainly it's Southern, and the classic dishes are served with a light touch and the freshest ingredients. The fried whiting and chicken are wonderfully crispy and not at all greasy, the garlic mashed potatoes and mac and cheese gloriously rich, the

cornbread airy and sweet. On weekend nights you can sit in the back room and watch a movie on a 64-inch television screen while you dine. The decor is pleasant and light-filled—nothing fancy—but the cooking is truly elegant.

327 Stuyvesant Avenue, Bedford-Stuyvesant
718-574-3728
Subway: A to Utica Avenue

Nordic Delicacies

Sometimes a person's just gotta have reindeer meatballs and *fiskpudding*. When Scandinavian cravings strike, head for this restaurant, one of the few gustatory remnants of Bay Ridge's substantial Scandinavian community. You can also buy prepared food to take home, as well as trolls and Norwegian sweaters. Afterwards, stop by **Leske's Bakery**, 7612 Fifth Avenue, and pick up a delicious, licoricey limpeh bread.

6925 Third Avenue, Bay Ridge, 718-745-3939
Subway: R to Bay Ridge Avenue

Pho Hoai

Fresh seafood and everything-but-the-kitchen-sink soups are our favorites at this pleasant, spacious, Vietnamese place. We especially like the fried crabs, the fresh (not fried) spring roll, and the clams in coconut juice—by the way, the clams are actually mussels. The detailed menu contains some wonderful descriptions, such as "(Combination extra big bowl) Rice Noodles Beef Soup Six Differences Brisket, Navel, Frank, Omosa Tendon & Eye of Round." For your information, omosa tendon is tripe.

1906 Avenue U, Sheepshead Bay, 718-616-1233
Subway: D to Avenue U
A new branch of Pho Hoai has recently opened
at: 8616 Fourth Avenue, Bay Ridge,
718-745-1640
Subway: R to 86th Street

Go Fish:
Brooklyn FISHING Spots

The typical city-dwelling fisherman must go to lengths to satisfy his habit: expensive tackle, permits and licenses, travel to far-flung locales. Not so the Brooklyn angler. For that lucky man (or woman, but it's usually a man, isn't it?), choices abound.

Sheepshead Bay used to be a fishing village and still looks like one—if your typical fishing village had a zillion restaurants, a comedy club, and Loehmann's. At the marinas along Emmons Avenue, you can book a day's fishing on one of the fishing boats that still ply the deep waters offshore for porgies, blues, fluke, sea bass, and blackfish. The earliest boats head out before 7 A.M. and don't return much before 3 P.M., but during the summer months especially, you can sign on for half-day or evening cruises. Reservations are not required, but calling ahead is strongly recommended. The cost is less than you'd pay for a Broadway—or even off-Broadway—show, and the price includes rental of all equipment; plus,

you get to keep the fish.
Here are some boats
worth trying:

Flamingo III ties up
right off the Knapp Street
exit of the Belt Parkway
on the corner of Harness
Avenue, 718-763-8745. The Weigand family's first
Flamingo started fishing fifty years ago. Full-day fishing only, leaving at 6:30 A.M., returning 3 P.M., seven
days a week.

The **Dorothy B.** docks at Pier 6, Emmons Avenue, 718-646-4057. Captain Kevin Bradshaw is the
third generation of his family to sail from Sheepshead
Bay in a boat of this name; his grandfather started the
business in 1917. Whole- and half-day cruises, depend-
ing on time of year.

The Sea Queen IV, Pier 5, Emmons Avenue,
718-332-2423, offers half-day cruises from 8 A.M. to
noon and 1 P.M. to 5 P.M., and summertime night cruises, 6 to 10 P.M. This is a family-oriented boat, a happy
place for novices; the crew will even clean your catch
on the return leg for you. *Sea Queen IV* begins sailing
on St. Patrick's Day (which happens to be the first day
of flounder season) and stops on Thanksgiving, when
the catch is striped bass.

For those last-minute doodads that you realize
you've forgotten only as the boat's about to leave, our
sources recommend **Bernie's Fishing Tackle**, 3128
Emmons Avenue, 718- 646-7600.

Across Flatbush Avenue from Floyd Bennett

Field is picturesquely named **Dead Horse Bay** (used to be a glue factory there). It's not such a picturesque place. In fact, some regulars call it Medical Waste Bay, but the fishing is good: weakfish and striped bass in August, blues in September. This is part of Gateway National Recreation Area (see p.71), and a fishing permit is required. To get one, show up at the Ryan Visitors Center at Floyd Bennett with a fishing pole (minimum length: 7 feet), tackle box, check or money order for $25, and driver's license or other identification. Ask for a map, which indicates Gateway's other fishing areas. Call Floyd Bennett Field, 718-338-3799, for more information.

Directions: Since there's no subway here, you need to drive or take the Q35 bus from the intersection of Flatbush and Nostrand Avenues.

Six-acre **Canarsie Pier**, at the very foot of Rockaway Parkway, is a great spot for family fishing, especially in April and early May, when the early bluefish are running. Other times, you might pull in flounder, blackfish, and fluke. There are no swimmers to scare away the fish, and there's a restaurant and rest rooms right there. The pier's part of Gateway, but no permit is required to fish here. You do, however, have to submit to the occasional open-air classical music concert on Saturday afternoons in July and August. The pier is open 24 hours a day, seven days a week. Call 718-763-2202 for more information.

Subway: L to Rockaway Parkway,
then the B42 bus

Only a savvy few know that **Prospect Lake** in Prospect Park contains a healthy, stable population of largemouth bass, as well as many small and peppy species, like sunfish, that are easy and fun for beginners. Catch-and-release is strongly suggested, for the well-being of both the lake and your digestion. Anglers fifteen and younger will enjoy the **Prospect Park Annual Fishing Contest**, now in its fifty-second year. There are prizes for the biggest fish caught—and thrown back, natch. No permit required. Call 718-965-8954 for more information.

Subway: D, Q to Parkside Avenue. Enter the park through the pergola at the corner of Parkside and Ocean Avenues. The lake is dead ahead, over South Lake Drive and the Bridle Path.

You don't need a permit to fish off Coney Island's **Steeplechase Pier**, and there's no admission either, but the throngs of people and the condition of the water make catching anything unlikely. On the other hand, if you were serious about fishing, why would you come to Coney Island? People are the catch of the day here, in marvelous variety.

Subway: B, D, F to Coney Island/ Stillwell Avenue

Ah, FLATBUSH!

The name sounds like a joke, but the place is *home:* home to the earliest Dutch farmers and the wealthy suburban homeowners of the Victorian era, home to the young Woody Allen and to many of the fabled Dodgers. Small wonder that P. G. Wodehouse wrote a song called "Nestin' Time in Flatbush"—well, maybe not so small. Its sprawling mix of cultures—Orthodox Jews, Russians, Cambodians, Jamaicans, Trinidadians, Vietnamese—makes it probably the most cosmopolitan part of Brooklyn. Still, it feels domestic, with people out shopping, tending to their gardens, playing ball with their kids. The best place to experience the peaceful coexistence of old and new is at Flatbush and Church Avenues.

Rising over this busy intersection with its clothing stores and patty shops is the white octagonal spire of **Flatbush Dutch Reformed Church**. The oldest church in Brooklyn, it dates from 1759; the original church on this site was founded in 1654 by Peter Stuyvesant. The church is a beauty, made of horizontally placed gray stone, with Romanesque windows and doors. Inside, there are Tiffany windows. The peaceful graveyard is shaded by big trees, including a spectacular weeping beech called "the bell tree" because of its shape. Walk among the weathered stones and you'll see the old Dutch names: Cortelyou and Lefferts, Suydam and Martense. The eighteenth-century brownstone markers have held up best; the angels look as if they were carved yesterday. At the back of the churchyard is the elegant parsonage, dating from 1853. It's peeling and decrepit, but there's no hiding its beautiful Greek Revival lines and spacious porch.

Off East 21st Street, behind the church, are the extraordinary **Kenmore and Albemarle Terraces,** planned developments from 1916–20. These two quiet, dead-end streets are oases of beauty and calm. On Kenmore, notice the garages incorporated into the design.

Back on Flatbush Avenue, look into **Erasmus Hall High School**, New York's first chartered secondary school. In the courtyard behind the imposing facade, you'll find the original school, a diminutive white frame building that went up in 1786. Inside, it's a museum set up as the old school used to be, with climb-in beds for the students, classrooms, dining room, etc., and some Dutch furniture of the period. You can visit on Monday and Thursday mornings at 10.30 A.M. Call 718-282-7804 and a student will take you on a tour.

Just down Flatbush there's **Loew's Kings Theater**, with an extravagant terra-cotta facade and equally splendid flourishes within. Barbra Streisand once worked here as an usher. Now the theater is dark, but when you look at the theater, the church, the little terraces, and the school all so close together, you get a deep feeling of neighborhood, entrenched and abiding for hundreds of years.

★ Also founded by Peter Stuyvesant, the **Flatlands Dutch Reformed Church** continues today in an 1848 building at 3931 Kings Highway, and there are many Dutch graves in the churchyard.

890 Flatbush Avenue,
718-284-5140
Subway: D, Q to
Church Avenue

Fabulous
FLOYD BENNETT FIELD

Gateway National Recreation Area was created twenty-six years ago as one of the nation's first urban national parks. The experiment has been a huge success. Stretching over portions of three boroughs and two states, it's visited by seven million people annually. Brooklyn's most interesting link in the chain is **Floyd Bennett Field**, an abandoned airfield with Art Deco buildings. Once it saw various record-breaking flights, now it's the site of nature walks, antique car shows, you name it. It's a haunting place.

Built in 1931, the airfield became the scene of flights by pioneers such as Amelia Earhart, Howard Hughes, Beryl Markham, and Eddie Rickenbacker. It was from here that the fabled "Wrong Way" Corrigan set out for California and landed in Ireland by mistake, and it was in front of a Floyd Bennett crowd that General Francesco de Pinedo, attempting a record in 1933, crashed before takeoff and was incinerated. In recent years, the airport's been home to various subdivisions of the Coast Guard and the NYPD, and all that's left now are empty buildings, the underground tunnel used by passengers to get to their planes, and miles of runways sprouting grass.

But there's so much going on! In the Blue Nose hangar, you'll find volunteers from HARP (Historic Aviation Restoration Projects) tinkering with old planes. In August there's the Brooklyn County Fair, with pig racing, and also contests involving large zucchini, and the consumption of Junior's cheesecake and egg creams made with Fox's U-Bet Syrup. And then there's the Music and Air Fair (when the old planes get trundled out), kite flying, model jet plane rallies (complete with heart-stopping crashes), cycling and Rollerblading on the runways, and tours of the control tower, hangars, and adjacent runways.

Nature has begun to reassert itself here. Spaces between the runways have returned to grassland full of wildflowers and grasshoppers, meadow voles, and mice; birds of prey search here for meals. The so-called "North 40" area has a nature trail where Rangers lead hikes. Over 180 species of bird have been officially recorded, including owls, egrets, ospreys, and many songbirds.

Floyd Bennett is the only place in the city where you can camp legally. Join one of the camp-out nights (bring your own tent) and listen to frogs and owls over the occasional siren and the roar of planes landing at Kennedy. Call 718-338-3799 for Floyd Bennett details.

★ The foot of Gerritsen Avenue, just nearby, is the site of an unusual seasonal pleasure: the annual **let's-watch-the-horseshoe-crabs-mating** walk led by the Park Rangers on a summer night. Call the Park Rangers at 718-438-0100 for information.

★ For **fishing** possibilities nearby, see p. 65 and for **miniature golf** see p. 86.

Directions: 2 or 5 to Flatbush Avenue/Brooklyn College, then the Q35 bus.

Buzz-a-rama 500, Gil Hodges Lanes,
Brownstone Billiards:
FUNKY FUN

Brooklyn, as writers Pete and Denis Hamill are only too happy to tell us, is gentrifying at an alarming rate. Not so long ago, they recall, Park Slope itself was a dinosaur-infested swamp fit only for proletarian toughs like—well, like the Hamills. And *now* look! It is to sigh.

Despite the influx of latté-swillers, Brooklyn's got a ways to go before Coney Island gets Disneyfied or Peter Luger's waiters learn some manners. We're too proud of our byways and eccentricities ever to conform to some outlander's idea of propriety. Take these three establishments:

What could be more Brooklyn than a bowling alley (favorite recreational venue of Ralph Kramden, the ultimate Brooklynite) founded by a former Dodger? The **Gil Hodges Lanes** in far-off Marine Park is a treat worth the trip: a spacious, state-of-the-art establishment with sixty-four lanes, whose gutter guards (essential for kids) appear at the yank of a lever from one of the local youths who operate the joint. Serious baseball memorabilia decks the walls, there's a centrally located bar next to a well-lit snack bar service (nachos, fries, and dogs are the order of the day). Parking is a cinch; the place has its own lot.

Gil Hodges Lanes
6161 Strickland Avenue, 718-763-6800/3333
Directions: If you aren't driving, take the D train

to Avenue U, then the B3 bus to Mill Avenue; turn right, walk one block, turn right again on Strickland, and there you are. Nothing to it, right?

In the '60s, New York City boasted over forty slot-car establishments where kids (and the occasional grownup) could race the speedy little electrically controlled cars. Only one remains today, in Flatbush: **Buzz-a-rama 500**, a friendly shambles of a storefront that's been around since 1965. Slot-car racing involves a swooping, curving track with grooved lanes (the slots) and six-inch or so racing cars that hurtle around the track at frightening speed—if you've got the right car and the right touch. Buzz-a-rama has four

tracks, including one just for official competition. Get on the good side of the mellow owner, Frank "Buzz" Perri, and he might take his precious custom-built car out for a spin. Frank says the thing goes 100 miles an hour; we believe him. This place is great for kids' birthday parties, by the way.

Buzz-a-rama 500
69 Church Avenue, 718-853-1800
Subway: F to Church Avenue

Tucked under a movie marquee on the Flatbush Avenue edge of Park Slope is **Brownstone Billiards**—cavernous, subterranean, satisfyingly dark and dingy. Still, it's a family place. On weekends, parents and kids cluster around the tables, working on their ball placement and follow shots. In back are Ping-Pong and air hockey, up front are a couple of video games. Kid-size cues are available. To impress the little ones, take a turn on the billiard or snooker table. Who'll know if you're good or bad?

Brownstone Billiards

308 Flatbush Avenue, 718-857-5555

Subway: D or Q to Seventh Avenue

The Dead Really Do Know Brooklyn:
GREEN-WOOD CEMETERY

Q: What do Jean-Michel Basquiat, DeWitt Clinton, Joey Gallo, F. A. O. Schwarz, Currier (not to mention Ives), Charles Ebbets (as in Field), Lewis Comfort Tiffany (like the lamp), the inventors of the sewing machine (Elias Howe) and the safety pin (Walter Hunt), Lola Montez, the Brooks Brothers, and Leonard Bernstein have in common?

A: They're all resting in peace in **Green-Wood Cemetery.**

Decades before the big city parks existed, New Yorkers came to Green-Wood to experience fresh air and greenery without leaving town. Commissioned in 1838, Green-Wood was a bucolic alternative to grim, crowded city burial grounds, a sanctuary whose light, air, and space implied that death was not an end, but a harmonious reunification with nature. It also offered permanence at a time when urban growth encroached regularly on graveyards (one of Green-Wood's nine-teenth-century dignitaries lay in two other cemeteries before coming to his final rest). Pastoral and scenic, Green-Wood was meant to be welcoming, not grim.

It remains so. A visit to Green-Wood is anything but morbid. Its 478 acres of rolling hills, artful planti-ngs, and meandering walkways (bearing names like Sweet Gum Path) frame vistas of idyllic beauty. As you walk through the imposing Gothic Revival entrance gate at 25th Street, designed by Richard Upjohn, look up and spot the nests of parrots who've lived there for thirty years (see p. 102). Strolling around, you'll see an amazing range of statuary, from simple obelisks to imposing Egyptian-style mau-soleums. On Battle Hill, one of the highest spots in Brooklyn, the statue of the Greek goddess Minerva stands, arm raised in salute to her sister goddess in the harbor, the Statue of Liberty. The Battle of Brooklyn (see p. 87) raged right along Battle Pass, and Minerva commemorates the soldiers of the Maryland Brigade who fell in the action. Look through the little window in the door of copper magnate Marcus Daly's tomb and you'll see a Tiffany window inside. More modest, more affecting, the Alfred Van Derwerken Jr. memorial is a small stone carved to look like a tree stump, with the simple inscription, "He loved nature." Jane Griffith's beautifully detailed marble headstone depicts the last time her grieving husband saw her alive, on the steps of their Greenwich Village brown-stone. Saddest of all is the elaborate monument to

Charlotte Canda, a much-loved girl who was thrown from her carriage on the way home from her seventeenth birthday party (which is why the monument is seventeen feet tall). For decades, this was the most visited grave in New York City.

Green-Wood is private, but you can visit any day from 8 A.M. to 4 P.M. Six hundred thousand people are buried here, and individual graves are very hard to find unless you know roughly where to look (the map you can pick up at the entrance provides only lot numbers), so it's best to join a weekend guided tour.

✳ The miniature crystal palace on the corner of 25th Street and 5th Avenue is **McGovern Weir**, a florist; the building is said to be a relic of the St. Louis World's Fair of 1904.

✳ In contrast to grand Green-Wood, the tiny (27' x 55') **Revolutionary War Cemetery**, on a quiet corner in Bay Ridge, contains a mere handful of headstones, though forty members of a local family, the Barkaloos, and two Revolutionary soldiers are buried there. The **Old Gravesend Cemetery**, on Gravesend Neck Road is an evocative remnant of the community that was founded in 1643 by Lady Deborah Moody, an English Anabaptist fleeing persecution.

She allegedly lived across the street at number 17 (see p. 55). The graveyard is open only by appointment, but you can stand outside and gaze at its weathered stones (and those in the Van Siclen family plot next to it) while the F train rumbles along nearby, on the elevated track above MacDonald Avenue.

Green-Wood Cemetery
500 25th Street, 718-768-7300
For tours, call Brooklyn Center for the Urban
Environment (BCUE) at 718-788-8500
Subway: N, R to 25th Street

Old Gravesend Cemetery
Gravesend Neck Road bet. between MacDonald
and Van Siclen Avenues
To visit, call the Gravesend Historical Society,
718-375-6831
Subway: F to Avenue U

Revolutionary War Cemetery
Narrows Avenue and MacKay Place
Subway: R to Bay Ridge Avenue

You Say Promenade, I Say Esplanade (Both Are Correct!): The Brooklyn HEIGHTS PROMENADE

If the Brooklyn Heights Promenade looks familiar to you, it's because you've probably seen it in an ad. Photo crews are always shlepping their stuff around the place, and with good reason. It's one of the best city views in the world: the downtown skyline, chockablock with skyscrapers, framed by the graceful arc of the Brooklyn Bridge on the right, on the left by the Statue of Liberty, the Staten Island Ferry, and the wide water.

For the locals and those who make the trip to get

there, the Promenade is more than a pretty location. It's a retreat with a wide-ranging array of habitués. Workers from Montague Street lunch there when it's sunny;  senior citizens convene on benches, reading, doing crosswords, and shmoozing; Bible students from the nearby Jehovah's Witness Watchtower buildings study Scripture; amateur photographers and wedding parties abound. For Rollerbladers and joggers (famous local Norman Mailer used to be a regular), the Promenade is the longest straightaway around and there are no cars to worry about.

None to worry about, but plenty to hear. The Promenade sits on top of two levels of highway—the Brooklyn-Queens Expressway—and Furman Street, the service road for the piers when they were thriving. The omnipresent hum of traffic is the only indication that you're above the hated Expressway, whose construction decimated whole chunks of Red Hook and Sunset Park. The Heights was more than well treated by Robert Moses, the Expressway's impresario, but there were costs. The site of 1 Pierrepont Place, home of Henry E. Pierrepont and one of the grandest of all Brooklyn brownstones, is today the Pierrepont Playground—shaded, beautiful, and civilized. It's always busy but never loses its tranquil feeling. (Sources say it's the perfect place for small Brooklynites to learn to walk.) Numbers 2 and 3 Montague

Terrace remain; the *AIA Guide* calls them the "most elegant brownstones remaining in New York City." Those in the know call them the Kings.

At the top of the Promenade, the walkway curves away from the water. From here you can walk down a steep hill to Old Fulton Street. Despite the presence of Bargemusic, the River Cafe, and the Anchorage, a hint of the rough waterfront mood survives, a world away from the lofty prospect of Brooklyn Heights.

Promenade, Esplanade, whatever
Montague Street bet. Montague Terrace
and Pierrepont Place
Subway: 2, 3, 4, 5 to Borough Hall

Come On-A My House:
The HOUSE TOURS

Tours of historic homes are a great Brooklyn tradition. The neighborhoods and houses on show differ greatly, but what they have in common is a bursting sense of pride. You get a little map, people inside the houses are delighted to show you around, and with any luck, there will be refreshments in some church hall nearby. These are the best-established tours, in chronological order:

April—Victorian Flatbush
The sprawling brick and frame homes of Flatbush were

built by turn-of-the-century developers who trumpeted this prosperous suburb as "a realm of light and air." The homes, some very ornate, have been lovingly restored by families attracted by the size of the houses and the leafy, bucolic spaces around them. One was prominently featured in the movie *Sophie's Choice*.

Flatbush Development Corporation,
718-469-5064

May—Fort Greene, Brooklyn Heights, Park Slope

Fort Greene is one of the oldest black neighborhoods in Brooklyn and is currently the center of a creative and cultural renaissance. It's great for strolling, too, with its park and gracious brownstones (see p. 114).

Fort Greene Association, 718-237-9031

Brooklyn Heights has New York's greatest concentration of historic houses. The churches are beautiful, too (see p. 127). This tour is a rare opportunity to stick your nose into the homes of the truly wealthy.

Brooklyn Heights Association, 718-858-9193

Park Slope offers an eclectic jumble of late-nineteenth-century styles: tall brownstones, deep limestones

with room to spare, and over-the-top mansions resplendent with stained glass, carved wood, and gargoyles. The gardens and backyards are a particularly lovely feature.

Park Slope Civic Council,
718-832-8227

June—Prospect-Lefferts Gardens, Boerum Hill

So you've never heard of **Prospect-Lefferts Gardens**, but that doesn't mean that this peaceful neighborhood on the southeastern edge of Prospect Park isn't worth visiting. Many of the houses have wonderful Arts and Crafts interiors.

Lefferts Manor Association, 718-284-6210

Boerum Hill is smaller and less grand than its affluent neighbors, Brooklyn Heights and Cobble Hill, but some of its three-story houses date back to the 1840s, and their interiors vary from lovingly restored to determinedly modern.

Boerum Hill Association, 718-403-9866

October—Prospect Heights, Bedford-Stuyvesant

Just across Flatbush Avenue from Park Slope, **Prospect Heights** has traditionally been eclipsed by its swankier neighbor. It's beautiful, though, with immense houses and big gardens.

Prospect Heights House Tours, 718-783-6530

Jump at the opportunity to explore Brooklyn's Harlem. **Bedford-Stuyvesant** is a gracious old neighborhood with its carefully maintained brownstone blocks and occasional magnificent mansions.

Brownstoners of Bedford-Stuyvesant,
718-574-1979

Brooklyn Is for
K I D S : *The Rolodex*

The borough is full of families and old people and people who don't leave; some of them never even go into "the city" to visit.

The streets are busy with children riding their bikes and playing arcane street games that are often thought to be extinct —sewercide, stoop ball, two-square and, everywhere, hopscotch. Brooklyn is great for kids, and we have a fistful of addresses to prove it.

Amusement arcades

Faber's Arcade, Coney Island (see p. 48.) **Funtime USA,** 2461 Knapp Street, 718-368-0500. Kind of places kids love, parents don't. Laser games, video games, bring all your money.

Baseball artifacts

Stanley's Place, 329 Fifth Avenue, 718-832-0239. Sells Negro Baseball League memorabilia as well as T-shirts and hats.

Bowling

Gil Hodges Lanes (see p. 73.), 6161 Strickland Avenue, 718-763-6800/3333, not to mention **Melody Lanes,** 461 37th Street, 718-499-3848, both tested by generations of Brooklyn children.

Carousels

Prospect Park, 965-8999 (see p. 116)
B & B Carousell, Coney Island, (see p. 48)

Coffee shops
(the good kind, with milk shakes)

Three wonderful places are described on p. 131. They're **Dizzy's** at 511 9th Street, 718- 499-1966; **Tom's Restaurant**, 782 Washington Avenue, 718-636-9738; **Hinsch's Confectionery**, 8518 5th Avenue, 718-748-2854.

Comic book stores

St. Mark's Comics, 148 Montague Street, 718-935-0911, sister-ship to the one on St. Mark's Place in Manhattan. **Comics Plus**, 302 Seventh Avenue, 718-768-5681, has many vintage comics as well as new ones, and some cool action figures.

Crafts places

You know the deal: you choose a pot or piggy bank or picture frame, then you paint it. Then they glaze and bake it. And when you get it back, it looks great! **The Painted Pot**, 333 Smith Street, 718-222-0334 **Clay Play**, 229 Fifth Avenue, 718-398-7104

Dance programs and performances

Both of these places bustle with workshops, performances, and community spirit. **Gowanus Arts Exchange**, 421 Fifth Avenue, 718-832-0018. **Spoke the Hub Dancing**, 748 Union Street, 718-857-5158

Egyptian mummy

In residence, third floor, **Brooklyn Museum of Art**, 200 Eastern Parkway, 718-638-5000.

Fishing

There's far more to it than the Prospect Park Lake. See p. 65

See p. 65

Funfairs

Deno's & Astroland. For these two Coney Island parks, call 718-372-5159. **Nellie Bly Amusement Park**, 1824 Shore Parkway, 718-996-4002. It's a little shabby, but safe, and great fun for younger kids.

Giant turtle

Godzilla in the Japanese Garden at the **Botanic Garden** (see p. 28.), 1000 Washington Avenue, 718-622-4433

Ice cream

Peter's Ice Cream Cafe, 185 Atlantic Avenue, 718-852-3835. Small-town feel; homemade ice cream in many varieties (some a little weird). **Luna Park**, 249 Fifth Avenue, 718-768-6868. Victorianesque-looking place with homemade ice cream and lots of action (see Puppets, below). **Uncle Luigi's**, 363 Coney

Island Avenue, 718-435-9378. This hole-in-the-wall serves high-quality Italian ices and ice cream in fifty flavors, and counting. It's open late and seems very popular with cops.

Indoor play

Kids 'n Action, 1148 McDonald Avenue, 718-377-1818.
Rides, video games, and a jungle gym/obstacle course
area. If your kid loves to collect hundreds of tickets
to redeem for tacky little souvenirs (we never met
one who didn't), this is a place to keep in mind for a
rainy day.

Kite flying

Best in **Prospect Park's Sheep Meadow** and
in **Shore Road Park** near the Verrazano Bridge
(see p. 132).

Movies

Pavilion Theatre, 188 Prospect Park West, 718-369-
0838. Very family-friendly, and offers reduced prices
for kids at the first matinee of the day.

Miniature golf

Gateway Golf & Tennis Range, 3200 Flatbush
Avenue, 718-253-6816, Floyd Bennett Field. Way out
here, there's a breezy, spacious course with lots of
nodding pampas grass.

Museums

New York Transit Museum, Boerum Place and
Schermerhorn Street, 718-243-3060. Housed in an old
subway station; contains vintage subway cars and the
real cab of a city bus for pretend-driving. Nice gift
shop. **Brooklyn Children's Museum,** 145 Brooklyn
Avenue, Brower Park, 718-735-4400. Country's oldest
children's museum (founded in 1899), in futuristic

structure. Great water-play, lots of activities and performances, very hands-on. In the summer, a free shuttle
bus, the Trolley Express, runs every half-hour between
Grand Army Plaza and the museum. Call the museum
Hot Line at 718-735-4400 for details. **Harbor Defense
Museum**, at Fort Hamilton, Fort Hamilton Parkway,
101st Street, 718-630-4349. Military dioramas, cannons,
atmospheric setting (see p. 133). **New York Aquarium**,
Surf Avenue at West 8th Street, 718-265-3474 (see p. 98).
The Old Stone House, J. J. Byrne Park, 3rd Street
between Fourth and Fifth Avenues, 212- 726-8062. An
historic site (see p. 105) with an exhibit that recreates
the Battle of Brooklyn: maps and dioramas and occasional festivities as well as storytelling.

Outdoor play

Pierrepont Playground, Brooklyn Heights
Promenade at Montague Street (see p. 79).
Imagination Playground, Prospect Park at Lincoln
Road and Ocean Avenue. The most recently restored
of Prospect Park's playgrounds.

Parks programs

Call the **Park Rangers** at 718-438-0100 to find out
about nature walks, and other events in all the parks;
they're always helpful and informative

Pizza

In a borough drowning in "legendary" pizza, the kids'
vote goes to Park Slope's **Two Boots**, at 514 2nd Street
(718-499-3253), for tasty food, crayons, festive atmos-

phere, skillful and long-suffering staff, and the essential Kitchen-Viewing Area.

Also favored: **Grimaldi's Pizzeria** at 19 Old Fulton Street, 718-858-4300 (see p.53)

Pool

Brownstone Billiards, 308 Flatbush Avenue, 718-857-5555. Also has air hockey, table tennis, and video games (see p. 74).

Powwows

There are usually two or three a year in Brooklyn. Children are thrilled by the dancing and drumming and also by the feathery dream catchers, nifty spears, arrowheads, etc., for sale. Call **Manahata Indian Arts Council** at 718-499-0912/832-4884 to find out where they'll be. This number is liable to change; if it does, call Information.

Prospect Park

For general information on all sorts of park programs, call 718-965-8999. **Lefferts Homestead Children's Museum**, 718-965-6505, has crafts, storytelling, and games. **Pedal Boats** ($10 an hour), 718-282-7789. **Carousel** (see above). **Zoo** (see below).

Puppets

Puppetworks, 338 Sixth Avenue, 718-965-3391. Venerable, much-loved troupe performs classic fairy tales. **Luna Park**, 249 Fifth Avenue, 718-768-6868. Ice cream parlor and Puppetworks outpost. Also coffee, clowns, birthday parties.

Red Hook

Free, innovative programs for kids, in a remarkable location—the Lehigh Valley Railroad Barge #79, aka the **Hudson Waterfront Museum**, moored at the end of Conover Street (see p. 97). Call 718-624-4719 for details of Circus Sundays in June; Dancing in the Streets.

Riding

Kensington Stables, 51 Caton Place, 718-972-4588, close to Prospect Park. **Jamaica Bay Riding Academy**, 7000 Shore Parkway, 718-531-8949, in Marine Park, which has glorious trails and wildlife.

Sleepovers

Call the **Zoo**, the **Aquarium**, or **Floyd Bennett Field** (718-338-4306).

Storytelling

The Old Stone House, 212-726-8062; **Lefferts Homestead Children's Museum** and **Imagination Playground**, Prospect Park, 718-965-6505

Skating

Wollman Rink, Prospect Park, 718-287-6431

Slot-car racing

Buzz-a-rama 500, 69 Church Avenue, 718-853-1800 (see p. 74)

Swimming

Metropolitan Pool, 261 Bedford Avenue, 718-599-5707. Immaculately renovated pool in Williamsburg with a glass skylight-roof and pretty tiling. Clean, airy, run by the Parks Department. You have to become a member to swim there (small fee).

Theater/dance

Brooklyn Academy of Music, One Hanson Place, 718-636-4111. Some extraordinary programs for families. **Brooklyn Center at Brooklyn College,** 718-951-4500. High-quality performing-arts productions from around the world.

Weirdo novelty shops

The Scouting Party, 135 Windsor Place, 718-768-3037, and its upstart rival close by, **Lucky Bug,** at 438 Seventh Avenue, 718-832-6601. Both excellent for purple hair dye, glow-in-the-dark stuff, and strange, tiny things.

World's oldest subway tunnel

Call the **Brooklyn Historic Railway Association** at 718-941-3160 for tour schedules.

Zoo

Prospect Park Wildlife Center, 718-399-7339, varied environments, accessible exhibits, very kid-friendly, especially the prairie dogs.

Where to Find Antiques, Almost-Antiques, and Trendy Knickknacks:
LOOKING FOR TREASURE

Desperate for cast-iron banisters or antique chairs? Maybe some '50s tablecloths or a vintage cocktail shaker? Brooklyn is full of places to find them, usually cheaper than in Manhattan.

Atlantic Avenue has traditionally been the place to start, and you can still find good things there, although you have to beware of crafty reproductions. **Time Trader Antiques** is a trustworthy place for solid, mostly turn-of-the-century, furniture in oak, mahogany, or walnut. Everything here is dated (as close as they can get). A couple of blocks away, the eccentric **Olde Good Things** (which also has a branch on West 24th Street in Manhattan), offers oddments—marble mantles, stained-glass windows, claw-foot bathtubs, hinges, handles, and ornamental wrought iron. It's as much fun as a flea market and more rewarding to poke around in, particularly if you're renovating.

Williamsburg is turning into a mini-mecca for people who want to deck their homes with hip or

unconventional items. **The Landmarks Preservation Commission's Architectural Salvage Warehouse** holds pieces of New York City buildings until someone comes along to offer them a good home. In this vast and shabby place you'll find chunks of plaster ornamentation, maybe a complete elevator cab, wainscoting, doors, sinks, toilets, spindles, and occasionally some porch columns or a pair of pews. The prices are great. Close by on Bedford Avenue, **Ugly Luggage** has furniture and kitschier items like trading cards and lunch boxes. The hip new **R**, on Wythe Avenue, is a good source for post–World War II furniture in good condition (whole lotta Eames chairs), and on the same block you'll find several other antique/used furniture/kitsch emporia.

In **Carroll Gardens**, the newly gussied-up stretch of Smith Street, north of Union Street, features a sweet, smart design place called **Astroturf**, whose owners have an excellent eye for retro weirdness. You'll find '50s lamps, all kinds of china, dressers, chairs, and many important paint-by-numbers pieces. Nearby, in **Cobble Hill**, you can recover from your search with an iced latté in the cafe at **Shakespeare's Sister**, where you'll find an excellent selection of cards, books, candles, and soothing soaps.

Finally, there's **Park Slope**. At the south end, check out the new **Blum County**, whose owners, the Blum sisters, have assembled an imaginative assortment of art, antiques, and furnishings (tea towels silkscreened with '50s motifs, giant iron newel posts turned into candlesticks). **Mostly Modern**, across the street, offers a serious reappraisal of the clunky lamps and furnishings that you were glad to leave behind at your parents'. On Fifth Avenue, **Flux & Co.** has a large collection of charming design flotsam and very little junk.

Atlantic Avenue
Time Trader, *368 Atlantic Avenue,*
718-852-3301
Olde Good Things, *400 Atlantic Avenue,*
718-935-9742
Subway: 2, 3, 4, 5, D, Q to Atlantic Avenue;
B, M, N, R to Pacific Street

Williamsburg
Landmarks Preservation Commission
Architectural Salvage Warehouse,
337 Berry Street, 718-487-6740. Hours vary,
so make sure to call.
Ugly Luggage, *214 Bedford Avenue,*
718-384-0724
R, *326 Wythe Avenue, 718-599-4385*
Subway: L to Bedford Avenue

Carroll Gardens
Astroturf, *290 Smith Street, 718-522-6182*
Subway: F to Carroll Street

Cobble Hill
Shakespeare's Sister, *270 Court Street,*
718-694-0084

Park Slope
Blum County, *396A Seventh Avenue,*
718-768-2586
Mostly Modern, *383 Seventh Avenue, 718-788-6230*
Flux & Co., *194 Fifth Avenue, 718-638-2633*
Subway: F to Seventh Avenue; for Flux, 2, 3 to
Bergen Street

A Tree Grows in Brooklyn— In Fact, Many Do:

MAGNOLIA TREE EARTH CENTER

The tree commemorated in Betty Smith's classic novel *A Tree Grows in Brooklyn* is the ailanthus, the pushy denizen of abandoned lots throughout the city. Smith's ailanthus grew in Williamsburg, but all over the borough, trees and gardens are a symbol of pride and community.

One of Brooklyn's most celebrated trees is a lofty southern magnolia that grows in front of a brownstone in Bedford-Stuyvesant. There's a story behind it, the story of Hattie Carthan (1901–84). An accomplished and charismatic African-American woman living in Bedford-Stuyvesant, she mobilized to save her neighborhood as it began a dramatic deterioration in the 1960s. She organized neighbors, block by block, she held parties and pig roasts, and she put the money she raised into a fund for new trees for the streets. The result: 1,500 trees, and 100 block associations.

Next, she took charge of a rare forty-foot magnolia grandiflora that had been brought to the area from North Carolina in 1885. The brownstones behind it, which protected it from the wind, were scheduled for demolition. Carthan went to war, and not only

was the tree saved, it was declared a living landmark. In short order, the three brownstones were land-marked, too, and they became the home of the **Magnolia Tree Earth Center**, the fulfillment of Carthan's dream—a community, environmental, and cultural center that teems with optimism and energy.

★ Every few blocks in Brooklyn, it seems there's a communi-ty garden or organized planting up and down the street. Two of the prettiest blocks are Vanderveer Place between Flatbush Avenue and E. 23rd Street, and Howard Avenue between Blake and Dumont Streets.

> **Magnolia Tree Earth Center**
> *677 Lafayette Avenue, 718-387-2116*
> *Subway: G to Bedford-Nostrand Avenues;*
> *A to Utica Avenue*

Beyond the Biggies:
Brooklyn's Little MUSEUMS

The Brooklyn Museum of Art, BAM, and the Botanic Garden are not the sum and substance of Brooklyn's cultural resources. Numerous smaller institutions flourish here, too, and they're often the result of some-one's preoccupation with a particular—sometimes very particular—subject. Brooklyn would be dimin-ished without the efforts of these noble obsessives.

Kurdish Library and Museum
Enter this elegant Prospect Heights brownstone and

you enter another world. Mannequins in brilliantly colored waistcoats, billowing pantaloons, and wrapped headdresses stand guard in the parlor. In glass cases are hand-carved pipe bowls, jewelry, musical instruments, and textiles. A tufted leather sofa sits next to floor-to-ceiling curtained shelves stuffed with books in many languages. This is the largest repository of Kurdish artifacts, books, and documents—not to mention slides, videos, and audiotapes—in the Western Hemisphere, a target destination for scholars, visitors, and expatriates of Kurdistan. Founded in 1981 by Vera Beaudin Saeedpour, the collection has been growing ever since, often at personal risk to contributors who've smuggled books and artifacts out of Turkey, Iran, and Iraq.

> *144 Underhill Avenue (corner of Park Place)*
> *718-783-7930, e-mail: kurdishlib@aol.com*
> *Subway: 2, 3 to Grand Army Plaza*

The Enrico Caruso Museum of America

This place is the expression of Aldo Mancusi's lifelong passion for the Neapolitan tenor. Mancusi grew up listening to Caruso and has been collecting memorabilia for decades. He opened his museum in 1992 and lives below the duplex that houses his vast collection of posters, photographs, documents, vintage Victrolas, caricatures drawn in Caruso's own hand, even his costume from *Rigoletto*. Mancusi owns every one of Caruso's 262 recordings and a silent film in which he starred. When you visit, be sure to see the eight-minute video that Mancusi put together. In 1997, the

Italian government granted Mancusi the honorary rank of *Cavaliere Ufficiale*. Call the *Cavaliere* for an appointment.

1942 East 19th Street, 718-375-8549
Subway: D, Q to Kings Highway

Lesbian Herstory Archive

The world's largest collection of lesbian-related material, this includes about 10,000 volumes, manuscripts, pulp paperbacks, and periodicals. Its Park Slope headquarters contains reading rooms and galleries. A lecture and discussion series called "At Home at the Archives" occurs every few months.

P.O. Box 1258, New York, N.Y. 10116
718-768-3953 (call for an appointment
and directions)
http://www.datalounge.net/network/pages/lha//

Hudson Waterfront Museum

David Sharps, clown and juggler, is also a devoted student of the golden age of New York's waterfront. That's why he spent two years pumping mud out of a derelict barge on the Jersey side of the Hudson. The barge, caulked and painted deep red, is now berthed in Red Hook (see p. 121), down the street from a lot where towed automobiles end up. Inside its barnlike cabin, small boats and obscure seafaring implements hang from the walls and rafters. During spring and summer, Sharps and colleagues present children's shows on board. The charming and amiable Mr. Sharps is full of tales of the New York waterfront. And with its sweeping vista of the harbor, the ferries, and the Statue of Liberty, the barge has probably the best view of any museum in the city.

Garden Pier 45

290 Conover Street, 718-624-4719

Directions: A, C or F to Jay Street/Borough Hall, then the B61 bus to Conover Street; or F or G to Smith-9th Streets, then the B77 bus.

Waterworld:
NEW YORK AQUARIUM
(It's Better Than the Movie)

The location of the New York Aquarium makes it special. Whether you come from the creaky old Coney Island subway station or by car, once you cross Surf Avenue all you can think about is the wide expanse of boardwalk, sand, and sea in front of you. Then, to enter the Aquarium, so close to the water, and see its extraordinary collection of sea life, is a real thrill. Try to visit on low-trafficked days (New Year's Day, for example) or very early in the morning. Otherwise you'll find yourself dodging the throngs of schoolchildren and weary, stroller-pushing parents.

A major attraction is the newly completed Sea Cliffs section, where penguins, seals, walruses, and otters lounge and flop around at close range. The keepers who feed them are friendly and knowledgeable. You can view the creatures from beneath the waterline and

see how graceful they look in their natural habitat. The beluga whales are enchanting for all ages—currently six whales are in residence, and you are cautioned to be quiet so as not to scare the babies. The fun of watching them is both simple and profound. "Wow!" you'll say as a vast white shape slips by, just inches away from your nose; "Wow!" again, as you hear them communicating to each other with their mysterious clicks. If there are kids in your party, take them to Discovery Cove, which has touch-tanks and, most thrillingly, a wave that crashes over their heads (behind glass). Don't miss the sharks, which look as menacing as they're supposed to, or the obliging dolphins, leaping to order. In the spring of 1998, a twenty-two-pound lobster, saved from dinner by the softhearted owners of the Old Homestead restaurant, joined the party.

The cafeteria is serviceable, but who cares, since Nathan's (see p. 59) is close by, just down Surf Avenue?

New York Aquarium
Surf Avenue at W. 8th Street,
718-265-3474
Subway: D, F to West 8th Street/
New York Aquarium

We Love the
NIGHTLIFE,
We Gotta Boogie: Brooklyn Gets Down

Brooklyn nightlife might sound like an oxymoron to some, but those people are bigoted and ignorant. Brooklynites do go out at night, in our way, and we have the venues to prove it. Popping up everywhere are hip cafe/bar/music/poetry joints where interesting-looking people lounge on dilapidated sofas. Here are some other ideas:

Vera Cruz in Williamsburg is a cramped, friendly bar shaped roughly like a toothpaste tube. On Monday nights at 8 P.M., there's Latin music and a vibrant Afro-Cuban scene, like a street corner in Havana. The music varies from rhumba to mambo to funky, and the so-called dance floor accommodates just a few virtuoso couples. The acoustics and quesadillas are great; so is the vibe.

195 Bedford Avenue, 718-599-7914
Subway: L to Bedford Avenue

You needn't worry about getting enough room to dance at **T. J. Bentley's** in Bay Ridge. It's a restaurant, and a very popular brunch spot, but dancing is the point. On Sunday and Wednesday evenings, you can hear big band music; on Fridays, a jazz-oriented quartet; and on Saturdays, "family-style music," i.e., '40s to contemporary whatever.

7110 Third Avenue, 718-745-0748
Subway: R to Bay Ridge Avenue

Russian nightclubs in Brighton Beach: They're legendary by now, rowdy places where you eat a multicourse meal (of which the appetizers are the best part) surrounded by intensely partying Russians in their sequins and shantung. You knock back vodka, experience a Vegas-type floor show, and if you've got the stamina, flail around on the dance floor under a mirrored ball. You'll need stamina because the air is blue with cigarette smoke, and the food is not what you'd call light. But this experience is a blast. It's said that the veteran **Primorski** has the best food but smallest dance floor. **Rasputin** is glamorous (you have to book way in advance), and the **Winter Garden** offers a winning combination of location (on the Boardwalk), excellent food (cherry dumplings, breast of duck), and a groovy floor show (with perfumed smoke). Wear all your jewelry!

Primorski, *282B Brighton Beach Avenue*
718-891-3111
Rasputin, *2670 Coney Island Avenue,*
718-332-9187
Winter Garden *3152 Brighton 6th Street*
718-934-6666
Subway: D, Q to Brighton Beach

Up Over Cafe is a small new jazz club up a flight of stairs on Flatbush Avenue. Performing there recently have been Michael Weiss, Naomi Johnson, and Cecil Payne. Cyrus Chestnut and Vincent Herring have appeared too. Order from the Wing Wagon downstairs when you get hungry, and bring your own alcohol. Up Over seats only about fifty, so advance booking is advised.

351 Flatbush Avenue, 718-398-5413
Subway: D, Q to Seventh Avenue

You Can't Make This Stuff Up:
ONLY IN BROOKLYN

Art for Heartburn's Sake

At the **Mill Basin Kosher Deli and Fine Art Gallery**
you can savor your brisket surrounded by lithographs
by Chagall and Mucha, original Ertés and Lichten-
steins, and more. The deli's Website posts images of
artworks for sale as well as pictures of house special-
ties like kasha varnishkes and pastrami. Go figure.

> **Mill Basin Kosher Deli and Fine Art Gallery**
> *5823 Avenue T , 718-241-4910*
> *http://www.webcom.com/ajarts/deli.html*
> *Directions: F or D to Avenue U, then the B3 bus*
> *west. Driving is easier.*

Da Boids

Several colonies of **parrots** thrive in Brooklyn. They're
called monk or quaker parrots, and as of this writing
twenty-two of them live in Green-Wood Cemetery's
Gothic Revival entrance gate. You'll see their elaborate
nests in and around the latticed stonework. Other
colonies near Brooklyn College have nests in the light
towers around the football field, on Bedford Avenue
between Avenues H and J, and at the corner of Ocean
Parkway and Foster Avenue. The origins of these immigrants are hazy. Some say they're descendants of a pair

that escaped from a crate at JFK; others cite an accident on the Brooklyn-Queens Expressway. It hardly matters; they're Brooklynites now.

Tall in the Saddle

You see them in Macy's Thanksgiving Parade, dashing in their satin jackets, ten-gallon hats, and flashy belt buckles. But more often you see the **Black Cowboys** riding the median on Conduit Avenue, the beaches near JFK Airport, sometimes even loping along in Prospect Park. They number about forty, and their stables are located near Linden Boulevard on the Brooklyn-Queens border; locals call the area Cowboy Town. The Cowboys see themselves as role models and in that capacity, they do charity benefits and workshops full of cowboy lore for children. But mostly they are simply present, dignified and skillful, where you'd least expect a cowboy to be. Border war between Queens and Brooklyn is not likely while the Black Cowboys are on patrol.

Sewer-side

It'll never be as popular as the Park Slope House Tour, but the **Coney Island Sewage Treatment Plant**, at Knapp Street and Avenue Z, receives visitors once a year, too. This is a state-of-the-art facility, as it should be, since it's the only such plant in New York surrounded by residential areas. For a more nautical experience, enjoy a boat ride on the notoriously stinky, hundred-year-old **Gowanus Canal**, said to be the watery grave of untold bad guys. Help is on the way here, we're told. A propeller-driven "flushing tunnel," built at the Canal's north end in 1911 but out of service since the '60s, is to be restarted this year. Neighbors are hopeful that contaminants and gunk will be washed out to dissipate in the harbor. We say, don't hold your breath, hold your nose.

Coney Island Sewage Treatment Plant
Knapp Street and Avenue Z, 718-743-0990
Subway: D, Q to Sheepshead Bay
(and a hefty walk)
Gowanus Canal Tour
For information, call Brooklyn Center for the Urban Environment (BCUE) at 718-788- 8500.

A Billboard of One's Own
For years passersby have wondered about the **witty billboard** that faces west on Atlantic Avenue at Nevins Street. The '50s-ish signs there look like ads, but they tout things like plates, cash, and penmanship. Turns out to be the ongoing project of **Jerry Johnson**, an artist/adman with a sarcastic sense of humor. Warning: It is unsafe to laugh too hard while operating a moving vehicle. Pull over.

Dutch Bums
Only in Brooklyn can you visit a Dutch stone house that was built in 1699, fought over during the first bat-

tle of the Revolutionary War, used as a clubhouse by the original Brooklyn (Trolley) Dodgers in 1883, and is now sweetly reconfigured as a museum and story-telling place for children. It's called **The Old Stone House** and it sits in J. J. Byrne Park at 3rd Street and Fourth Avenue in Park Slope.

> *212-726-8062 (headquarters of the First Battle Revival Alliance)*
> *Subway: M, N, R to Union Street;*
> *F to Seventh Avenue*

PALATIAL INSTITUTIONS:
The Williamsburgh Savings Bank Tower and Others:

Driving around Brooklyn, you're likely to come upon some massive building swarming with Romanesque turrets, cupolas, columns, or gargoyles. Then you're past, wondering what the heck it was. Here are a few of the borough's most fabulous edifices:

Banking on Brooklyn

Brooklyn's endless banks and churches convey the solid bourgeois pride of the late nineteenth century and the banks are actually churchlike in their money-worshiping splendor. The most spectacular, visible for miles around, is the **Williamsburgh Savings Bank Tower** on Hanson Place, built in 1929. No longer the tallest structure in Brooklyn (that's a transmission tower on top of Brooklyn Technical High School), it's still the tallest building, at 512 feet. Brooklynites love it passionately for its great illuminated clock (by which so many of us set our watches), its streamlined shape, its carvings, statues, and its ornate lobby—less so for the concentration of dentists who, strangely, have offices there. Nearby, in Fulton Mall, there's the **Dime Savings Bank** (1907) built in the Roman Revival style with a dome and columns and spectacular gilded dimes in the interior. In Williamsburg itself, another domed cutie is clearly visible from Manhattan —the **Williamsburgh Savings Bank**. Look for it as you cross the Williamsburg Bridge.

Our Frank

Three of the borough's finest Victorian buildings are the work of Frank Freeman. He designed the **Herman Behr House** in Brooklyn Heights (see p. 35) and the **Eagle Warehouse** on Old Fulton Street. The Eagle Warehouse is a wonderful, medieval-looking pile with extraordinary bronze lettering and ironwork, built in 1893 and named after the *Brooklyn Daily Eagle*, the famous newspaper which once had a printing plant on this site. The building is condominiums now, and some lucky soul has the top-floor apartment behind the glass face of the clock. A year earlier, Freeman built what used to be the **City of Brooklyn Fire Headquarters** right in the middle of downtown Brooklyn. You can recognize his style in the massive arched entranceway; above the arch its architecture soars vertically, like a slightly sedated version of a fanciful Rhine castle.

It's true. They don't make'em like they used to.

★ The main branch of the Brooklyn Public Library (1941), by Grand Army Plaza, with its lofty sayings and gilded Egyptian carvings on the facade, is a mighty monument to the power of the word. It has recently been landmarked.

Williamsburgh Savings Bank Tower
One Hanson Place at Ashland Place
Dime Savings Bank of New York
9 DeKalb Avenue (off Fulton Street)
Williamsburgh Savings Bank, *175 Broadway*
Eagle Warehouse & Storage Company
28 Old Fulton Street
City of Brooklyn Fire Headquarters
365–367 Jay Street
Brooklyn Public Library
Grand Army Plaza at the intersection of
Flatbush Avenue and Eastern Parkway

Attention,
PARK SLOPE
Shoppers!

Park Slope's Seventh Avenue is like the main street of a small town populated largely by writers, vegetarians, lesbians, and shiny new families with comfortable incomes. You can still find old-style bakeries and stationery stores in among the tony coffee joints (one per adult resident), and some of the shops are worth a visit.

Starting at the Flatbush Avenue end, you've got:

Hooti Couture. Cute and kitschy, heavily '50s-inspired, and crammed with cocktail glasses, costume jewelry, vintage party dresses, plastic handbags, and flower vases. Owned by a flamboyant, charming Southerner—who may cut you a deal if she's in a good mood.

179 Berkeley Place, 718-857-1977

Zuzu's Petals. Fonda, a smart, opinionated lady, has been selling plants and flowers here for twenty-five years. The locals love her glorious arrangements for parties and the high-quality bedding plants she offers through the spring and summer. The loose flowers are expensive but top-quality, and so are the heavenly French soaps.

81A Seventh Avenue, 718-638-0918

Leaf 'n' Bean. This Slope institution takes its coffee and its customers seriously. When the staff recommends the Sumatra Mandheling, go for it. You can also find good loose tea (particularly the Ceylon Ultima), cool mugs, jams, hot sauces, candlesticks, and such. House-gift central. (There's another branch on Montague Street in Brooklyn Heights.)

83 Seventh Avenue, 718-638-5791

The Park Slope Food Coop

They won't allow any old frivolous, casual types to

shop in there, but you can look, you can dream. Twenty-five years old, the coop offers great stuff at reasonable prices to the 5,500 members who toil there a couple of hours every month, as well as a website and a newsletter, *The Linewaiters Gazette*. Also online is Josh Karpf's *Tales from the Coop*, a glimpse of the coop's vivid inner life (see p. 143).

782 Union Street, 718-622-0560

The Community Bookstore

Will this literary place survive the crushing attack of Barnes & Noble six blocks away? Nobody knows, but the store has boosted its lineup of readings, set up great discounts, a cafe, and a garden out back where you can read to the gentle burbling of a waterfall. (Don't step on the resident frog.) So buy a book! Support the plucky independent!

143 Seventh Avenue, 718-783-3075

The Clay Pot (see p. 50)

Little Things

Park Slope's most prominent citizens are its children, and Little Things aims to supply them with all the toys, craft kits, and Beanie Babies their little hearts desire. The store's lavender awnings are everywhere, but the branch to visit is two doors down from the Clay Pot (see p. 50). In addition to toys, it stocks Sportsac bags and backpacks, flowing hippiesque clothing, and lots of delicate, inexpensive jewelry, which makes it a magnet for teenage girls.

166 Seventh Avenue, 718-768-1014

Barnes & Noble

You can browse, read a magazine over coffee, buy a book at a great price, and your kids can have a wonderful time in the huge, welcoming children's section. Surely there's room for both this and the Community Book Store.

267 Seventh Avenue, 718-832-9066

For antiques and kitsch, try **Blum County** and **Mostly Modern** (see p. 92).

Last Exit Books is on Sixth Avenue. Alan, the owner, seems actually to have read many of the secondhand books he sells. Particularly strong in philosophy and belles lettres, this is a browser's delight.

447 Sixth Avenue, 718-788-6878

John Morisi and Sons

Further down the Slope, this family business has been making extraordinary pasta since 1940 (with equipment made in 1913!). Flavors (all natural) range from saffron and pepper (black, chili or jalapeño) to wine and prune (not a typo). Shapes include spacarelli, bumbola, occhi di lupo and sciafatoni. Morisi's dense pasta takes a while to cook, but a pound will feed four adults and it's deliciously worth the wait.

186 Eighth Street (Between Third and Fourth Avene), 718-788-2299

N.B. There are splendid mansions and brownstones all around you in Park Slope. It's generally agreed that the most marvelous blocks are **Carroll Street** between Eighth Avenue and Prospect Park West and **Montgomery Place**. And remember, the glorious park is just two blocks above Seventh Avenue. You can get the makings of a great picnic at the **New Prospect at Home** (52 Seventh Avenue, 718-230-8900) and go sprawl on the grass.

> *Subways: D train to Seventh Avenue (at*
> *Flatbush Avenue); F train to Seventh Avenue*
> *(at Ninth Street); 2, 3 to Grand Army Plaza*

The Power of Pratt: The Engine Room at
PRATT INSTITUTE

Ever since its construction in 1887, Pratt Institute's Engine Room has been more than a power plant; it's been a place to see and be seen. In the early days, ladies and gentlemen from the mansions on Clinton Avenue would promenade along the gallery in their weekend finery, watching the engines work. There was no cable then, of course, but even now the Engine Room is a campus landmark and meeting place, not to mention the site of one of Brooklyn's most unusual New Year's Eve celebrations (see p. 32).

There's one very good reason why this place is so loved: the beautiful Ames Iron Works steam engines, circa 1900. They are massive and curvy, painted a deep burgundy with gold trim, and illuminated by the enormous gilt chandelier that hangs in the center of the room, at just about eye level for the gallery. Every surface in the place seems to have just been polished and dusted—except on the gallery, that is, where an indeterminate number of cats congregate, grooming themselves, eating and drinking from the dishes left out for them, lolling in the reassuring, humming warmth of the place. Look on the far wall of the gallery for a memorial to one of the Engine Room's beloved feline occupants, Eva Braun (1970–85).

But the Engine Room wasn't always a showplace. By the late '40s, the growth of alternating current made the engines obsolete. Boiler steam still heated the dorms, but the engines were allowed to deteriorate. By 1965, the great viewing windows had been blacked out.

Then Conrad Milster, cat fancier and self-described "preservationist of mechanical artifacts," became Chief Engineer. He cleaned the windows, hung the chandelier, painted the engines and got them up and running again. He has also turned the Engine Room into an informal museum of machinery. On the walls are a sign from the DeLavergne Refrigerating Machine Company and one from Ruppert's Brewery that reads "NO LOAFING." In a glass case is the movement from the old brewery's tower clock. It's a warm place in every sense of the word. The staff are friendly. Students between classes play with the cats. Considering their beauty and age, it's easy to forget that these engines still provide about a third of the power consumed on the Pratt campus.

★ While you're in the neighborhood, take a look at the enormous Italianate mansion at 232 Clinton Street. It belonged to Charles Pratt (founder of the Pratt Institute), and he erected three across the street for his children (lucky kids!), at numbers 229, 241, and 245. They vary greatly in style, but not in grandeur. Frederic's, at 229, boasts a colonnaded pergola, and Charles's at 241, with its wide arched entry, is now the residence of the Bishop of Brooklyn.

*Subway: G to Clinton-Washington Avenues
or Classon Avenue*

Not Forgotten:
The PRISON SHIP MARTYRS' MONUMENT, Fort Greene Park

Walt Whitman was here, agitating. The editor of the *Brooklyn Daily Eagle*, he had a platform to make his views felt, and he felt very strongly that the people of this cramped shantytown needed a park. After his lengthy campaign, Washington Park (later Fort Greene Park) was finally built, in 1850. It was redesigned in 1867 by Olmsted and Vaux, and their work survives today. But the park's most interesting and visible feature is the **Prison Ship Martyrs' Monument.**

This great column commemorates the awful deaths of 11,500 American soldiers who were imprisoned on wrecked and rotting British ships moored just off the shoreline during the Revolutionary War. Their bodies were treated as brutally as they had been when

alive, tossed overboard or buried in shallow graves by the shore. Over the years, the bones kept washing up, and public sentiment mounted for some kind of memorial. In the 1870s, twenty slate boxes of bones were interred in a vault, but it wasn't until 1907 that enough money was raised for the memorial. It stands as the world's tallest Doric column, and a powerful reminder of Brooklyn's past.

★ **Fort Greene** itself is in a happy state of flux today; the whole area is going through a rebirth. Home to artists, writers, musicians, and movie people, it's full of African-American-inspired restaurants, cafes, and stores. We recommend **Cambodian Cuisine** (see p. 26) or **Miss Ann's**, a minuscule place at 86 South Portland (718-858-6997), which offers sublime Southern food. On Fort Greene's southwestern edge sits the Atlantic Center, part of the commercial revival that's storming through downtown Brooklyn. Certainly, you can buy some nice sneakers or a stereo there, but if you want to look at something pretty, turn away to the tranquil, tree-lined brownstone blocks between Lafayette and DeKalb Avenues. Our favorite is **South Portland Street**, leading up from Lafayette Avenue to Fort Greene park. The **Lafayette Avenue Presbyterian Church** is noted for its Tiffany windows (see p. 128). And there's the **Joseph Steele House**, a lemon-yellow frame house of surpassing prettiness at 200 Lafayette Avenue. The small east wing was built in 1812, the rest, thirty or so years later. It even has a widow's walk, for looking out at the harbor.

Subway: A to Lafayette Avenue; 2, 3, 4, 5
to Atlantic Avenue

Splendor in the Grass:
PROSPECT PARK

Everybody knows that Olmsted and Vaux regarded Prospect Park as their masterpiece, not that other park in Manhattan. We mean no disrespect to the other one; we are as fond of it as we would be of any perfectly rectangular green space surrounded by tall buildings that are always in view. It is simply not the sylvan retreat that Prospect Park is. Though smaller than the other one (526 acres as compared to 843), Prospect Park offers more varied and more isolated habitats, a boon to birders as well as the rest of us. Here are some other reasons why, in Brooklyn, Olmsted and Vaux got it right:

1) The park's front door, opposite Grand Army Plaza, is a truly majestic site. The **Soldiers' and Sailors' Memorial Arch**, flanked by circular walks, gardens, and a fountain, faces the classically inspired park entrance, designed by Stanford White. The imposing Brooklyn Public Library (see p. 107) is a suitably dignified complement. On spring and summer weekends, you can climb to the top of the Arch for a spectacular view of the city and harbor. (Call 718-965-8968 for details.)

2) The **Long Meadow** (best approached through the Endale Arch, to your left as you enter the park) is one of the only places in New York where grass and sky dominate the landscape as far as the eye can see. Believed to be the largest open space in any urban park in the country, it is six times larger than the other

park's Sheep Meadow, and far less likely to be overrun by Garth Brooks fans.

3) The carousel is New York's most beautiful and least expensive—it costs only 50 cents, compared to 90 cents for the one in Manhattan. The wait at Prospect Park's is rarely longer than five minutes and the thing spins *really* fast.

4) Prospect Park has no transverse, so automobiles can't zip through. The other has four, which means you're never very far from engine noise.

5) This is the only park in America that contains a genuine Dutch house that is also an interactive children's museum. The **Lefferts Homestead**, between the carousel and the zoo, was built in 1783, and it offers workshops, storytelling, and other kid-centric activities (see p. 88).

6) The serene, unobtrusive **Quaker Cemetery** near the 16th Street entrance predates the Park and is still in use; Montgomery Clift is buried here.

7) Prospect Park's playing fields are all toward the outer edges of the park, which makes them easy for athletes and spectators to reach without disturbing the woodsier interior. Sport and solitude coexist peacefully. And whom would you rather watch: natty West Indian cricketers in white flannels, or stagehands in *Cats* jackets playing softball?

8) "We must save it," Marianne Moore declared in her 1967 poem, "The Camperdown Elm." "It is our crowning curio." And it was saved. Moore galvanized money and support for the rare and ailing tree. A Scotch elm grafted to American elm that is over one

hundred years old, it resembles a large bonsai, sturdy and delicate. The **Camperdown Elm** thrives today, protected by a little wire fence, just south of the Boat House near Hill Drive. (Camperdown elms must be less curious now; you can buy them online.)

9) History happened here. Prospect Park's hills and dells are largely manmade, but Battle Pass, along the East Drive between the Vale of Cashmere and the Zoo, closely follows the road that ran between the towns of Flatbush and Brooklyn. One of the markers here commemorates the Dongan Oak, which was felled to impede the British advance. General Washington's troops bivouacked and briefly engaged the enemy here in August 1776 during the Battle of Brooklyn (see p. 87), the first and largest conflagration of the Revolutionary War.

10) Fewer is better. The **Prospect Park Alliance** estimates that 6 million people a year visit the park; the other's Conservancy estimates 15 million visitors. There are no statistics on how many of the latter are Garth Brooks fans.

N.B. The farmers arrive early every Saturday morning for the Greenmarket at Grand Army Plaza. Consider— it's a great place to get breakfast.

Prospect Park
Bounded by: *Park Slope (Prospect Park West),*

Windsor Terrace (Prospect Park Southwest),
Prospect Park South (Parkside), Prospect-
Lefferts Gardens (Flatbush Avenue)
Main entrance: *Grand Army Plaza,*
at the intersection of Flatbush Avenue
and Eastern Parkway
Other formal entrances: *at the intersection*
of Prospect Park Southwest and Parkside; at the
intersection of Parkside and Ocean Avenue;
at the intersection of Empire Boulevard and
Ocean Avenue
Maps: *Situated at entrances, and there are*
signposts throughout the park.
Subways: 2, 3, to Grand Army Plaza; F to 15th
Street/Prospect Park; D to Parkside Avenue;
D or Q to Prospect Park
Main information number for the Park:
718-965-8999

Note: *In the summer, a free shuttle bus runs*
between the park and the other cultural institutions
in the neighborhood (see p. 142).

RAILROAD MADNESS:
Atlantic Avenue Tunnel, Broadway Junction, and Train World:

For railroad enthusiasts (we know you're out there), Brooklyn holds a couple of extraordinary attractions: the world's oldest subway tunnel and the world's largest, most complex elevated junction.

The Atlantic Avenue Tunnel is easy to reach. Its excavated portion runs under Atlantic Avenue from Court Street to Hicks Street. Built in the 1840s to move freight  cars from waterfront ferry docks to rail connections downtown, the tunnel was in use less than twenty years before it was shut and sealed by a real estate developer hoping to turn Atlantic Avenue into the Champs-Élysées. It was reopened in 1916 after rumors that German-sympathizing anarchists planned to blow it up. Resealed, the tunnel was forgotten, but legends remained. Then Bob Diamond, an intrepid Brooklyn College student, heard the stories and set about tracking down the site. After months spent poring over nineteenth-century documents and pestering borough officials, in 1980 he finally got permission to go down a manhole at the intersection of Court Street and Atlantic Avenue. He broke through a wall and felt a cool breeze. Today, Diamond heads the Brooklyn Historic Railway Association, a fund-raising organization, and leads regular tours of the tunnel.

Diamond has big plans. His group is restoring derelict trolley tracks in Red Hook and they've acquired a couple of trolley cars. He envisions a trolley line beginning at Beard Street on the waterfront, connecting to the Atlantic Avenue tunnel, and ending downtown. Don't bet against it; he's tenacious.

In the meantime, contact the Brooklyn Historic

Railway Association to find out when Diamond's next tunnel tour is. He's a fascinating guide, whether explaining nineteenth-century tunnel-digging techniques or passing on stories of the tunnel diggers (like the one about the cruel foreman murdered, then mixed into the cement by his crew—"he's in the walls"). If you're claustrophobic, climbing through the manhole may present a moment's difficulty, but it's worth it. The tunnel is spectacular—cool, high and vaulted, and sepulchrally quiet despite the traffic above. This is a beautiful, strange sight; bring a flashlight and look for ancient graffiti, albino crickets, and old hardware.

Atlantic Avenue Tunnel *The entrance is situated in the middle of the busy Court Street/Atlantic Avenue intersection just below Brooklyn Heights. Tour groups meet outside the Independence Savings Bank on the southwest corner and, when the traffic lights change, walk over to the manhole.* **Brooklyn Historic Railway Association** *718-941-3160*

The **Broadway Junction—East New York elevated subway stop** is a more esoteric landmark. This astounding complex of platforms and passageways is formed by the intersection of the A, C, J, L, and Z subway lines and an LIRR branch line. In its heyday, three signal towers oversaw all the comings and goings; the skeletons of two of them, ghostly wooden sheds, still stand. For the best view, walk to the end of the L platform farthest from the stairs and look down. If the view makes you nervous, remember that most of what you're standing on has been in place since 1916. Unlike the tunnel, Broadway Junction is always open, but not long for this world, at least in this form. Several of the tracks are no longer in use, and there is sure to be some "rationalization" of the structure, i.e., replacement and removal. See this sight while you can.

Train World is the biggest train shop in New York City, cluttered and lots of fun to visit. Most customers here seem to be adult hobbyists, men beadily intent on enhancing their setups, and there is much banter between them and the friendly staff about sneaking new purchases past the wife. But kids starting out will find this place irresistible, too. It stocks everything from diminutive N-scale trains to the mighty G type. You can spend thousands on pricey collectibles, but simple starter sets (a circle of track, an engine, a few cars) can be had for $50 or so. For much less, you can acquire tackle that's crucial to the model railroader: smoke-producing fluid, extra track, tiny people and trees.

Train World, 751 McDonald Avenue
Kensington (part of Flatbush), 718-436-7072
Subway: F to Ditmas Avenue

RED HOOK'S
Resurrection

Go see this haunting place for the glorious light, deserted cobbled streets, incredible views, abundant space—and new resurgence.

The story so far

After the Second World War, the bustling Brooklyn waterfront began to fade as the new container ships went to New Jersey, taking the jobs with them. When Robert Moses built the Brooklyn-Queens Expressway, otherwise known as "the trench," it separated Red Hook from the shops, subway stops, and prosperity of Brooklyn and the world. Starved of life, the neighborhood withered.

The update

The artists arrived, attracted by low rents, light, and isolation. A local developer began to restore and rent out the gorgeous Civil War–era red-brick warehouses, hoping to create a working waterfront that would be hospitable to light industry as well as artists. Now, people have big plans—marinas, parks, boat-building, cruise ships—all of which could founder if the city brings a waste transfer station into the Erie Basin, subjecting the neighborhood to a steady stream of garbage trucks and barges, with their attendant noise, pollution, and stink. Best to get out to Red Hook as soon as you can.

The tour

Take a map and, for convenience, a car (parking is easy). Go south along Van Brunt Street until you get to Beard Street. The beautiful brick building in front of you is the **Beard Street Pier** (1869), circled by a brand-new public walkway. Go in through big iron gates—there's a front and back set, and one should be open. As you walk down the pier, look in through the great iron doors to see the lofty spaces and bustle inside. The trolley cars and tracks outside may one day connect Red Hook to the rest of Brooklyn, thanks to the efforts of the Brooklyn Historic Railway Association (see p. 120). Right at the end is a cheerful metal artwork and a breathtaking view out over the water. The Statue of Liberty! The Staten Island ferries! Tugs, barges, merchant ships! Ducks! Connoisseurs of urban decay will thrill to the sunken lightship with just its masts showing, the abandoned sugar works looking like an enormous upside-down kitchen funnel, and picturesquely rotting piers. Yet boats chug by, vans rumble in and out, people appear round corners. This old place is functioning.

At the end of Conover Street sits **Lehigh Valley Barge 79**, home of the **Hudson Waterfront Museum** (see p. 97). That's a beautifully maintained community garden right next to the water. Walk back up Conover Street and left on Coffey Street to the water. The block between Conover and Ferris Street is the prettiest in Red Hook, a reminder of the way things used to be. Down at the water there's a spiffy new park and a pier for fishing and lounging. Check out the spectacular warehouse at 480 Van Brunt Street, and three

grand old (c. 1860) buildings that once comprised the **Brooklyn Clay Retort and Firebrick Works.** (Look for a tall chimney and you'll find them, at 76–86 Van Brunt, 99–113

Van Dyke, and 106–116 Beard Streets.) That closed bar on Conover Street is the **Red Hook Yacht and Kayak Club**, otherwise known as Sunny's. It's open on Friday nights—and there you have the entire Red Hook nightlife scene.

Finally, go south on Columbia Street until it ends in a flurry of NYPD signs. A police car park occupies much of this scythe-shaped outer edge of the Erie Basin. But notice the nice new railings and benches on your left, facing Gowanus Bay. Sit for a while and soak up the life of the harbor.

★ The summer is a particularly festive time to visit. **The Brooklyn Waterfront Artists Coalition (BWAC)** holds a big show in the neighborhood in May, and the **Hudson Waterfront Museum** stages Saturday evening concerts, Sunday afternoon circus shows, and a children's dance festival ("Dancing in the Streets"). You can get to the jollity on the free Con Edison Showboat Shuttle, which stops at various Park Slope, Cobble Hill, and Brooklyn Heights locations. For BWAC, call 718-596-2507; for the museum and shuttle bus, 718-624-4719.

> *Directions: Take the A, C or F to Jay Street/Borough Hall, then the B61 bus to Conover Street, or the F or G to Smith-9th Streets, then the B77 bus.*

Earthly Delights:
SAHADI IMPORTING COMPANY, INC.

With its open sacks and barrels of grains and spices, its bulk containers of olives, nuts, and dried fruits, its mixed fragrance of cumin and coffee beans, and the beat-up dispenser from which customers must take a number during crowded times, this looks like an old place—and it is. The Sahadis have been doing business in Brooklyn for fifty years; the original Sahadi was established in Manhattan in 1898. Today the store anchors the Middle Eastern commercial enclave that flourishes along Atlantic Avenue between Court and Hicks Streets and includes restaurants, food and music stores, and the Damascus Bakery (on the avenue since 1936). Weirdly, this shopping district flourishes where there are no Middle Eastern residents to speak of. There used to be, of course: the merchants and work-men who moved to Brooklyn early in the century from the original "Little Lebanon" in lower Manhattan.

On any given day, Sahadi has on hand about a hundred fifty vari-eties of cheese (including some Lebanese and Syrian varieties you're not likely to find anywhere else in town), and several dozen types of olives and olive oils. There's every imaginable dried fruit, including bananas and strawberries; nuts both roasted and raw, salted and un-. There's *crecre*, Chinese peanuts with a flavored coating; weird herbs like sumac and *mahleb* (made from the inside of cherry pits, used to flavor the Syrian string cheese), and dried *mloukhiyeh*, a forbidding spinachlike vegetable used in soups and gravies. There's Afghan bread as big as a pillow case, Turkish delight studded with pistachios, and Jordan almonds. In the back, the prepared foods section offers superb hummus, baba ghannouj, tabbouleh, and also what experts—us, actually—believe to be the best kibbeh (ground lamb with pine nuts and spices) in New York.

Sahadi, unlike other gourmet shops, sells bulk food as well. As Charlie Sahadi says, "I can sell you five ounces of peanuts or a twenty-pound bag." Because the store is a wholesaler and distributor as well as a retailer, the prices are moderate to eye-poppingly low. Bear in mind, however, that Sahadi's range and quality is not exactly a state secret, so you'll have to wait your turn during the weeks before Thanksgiving, Christmas, or any other big food holidays. The consistently helpful and cheerful staff will answer your questions and let you taste an olive or a piece of cheese; they make it easy to remain patient.

Sahadi Importing Company
187–189 Atlantic Avenue
Edge of Brooklyn Heights,
718-624-4550
Subway: 2, 3, 4, 5 to Borough Hall;
F to Bergen Street

He Did Windows:
TIFFANY in Brooklyn

Louis Comfort Tiffany set up his studio in the 1870s and brought American stained glass into the forefront of the "art glass" movement, experimenting with layered glass fragments to create different textures and gradations of color. The windows he created were so three-dimensional that they appeared almost sculptural. By the early 1900s, he'd figured out how to produce thinner glass, which let in more light.

During the Brooklyn Heights building boom, Tiffany was kept busy making stained-glass windows for the new churches. There are Tiffany windows in several Brooklyn locations, but the Heights has the greatest concentration—more than two dozen! To see them, just call the churches beforehand. If you're lucky, someone knowledgeable will show you around. A donation will be appreciated.

The First Unitarian Church (1844) is the real prize, a Gothic sandstone pile which celebrated its fiftieth anniversary by commissioning a set of windows from Tiffany. In the sanctuary there are ten, as well as the rose window, and two in the adjoining chapel, used today as a Sunday school. The sanctuary has a gallery, which splits the windows, but its advantage is that you approach the upper windows and see them up close. Look at the thickness of the angels' pearly robes and the way the faces look illumined. Downstairs, don't miss the forest scene, with a brook and the trees reflected in it. The range of techniques and styles here is a testament to Tiffany's versatility. If you're lucky, Ron McFarlin, who works at the church, will show you around, lucidly explaining just what those glass artists of a hundred years ago were doing.

Try to see **First Presbyterian** (1846), too. The *River of Life* window required so much cobalt blue that the church had to pay extra. *At Evening Time It Shall Be Light* is a radiant golden evening in wooded hills, and there's a glorious mosaic skylight in the Arts and Crafts style. **Plymouth Church** (1847) has five Tiffanys in Hillis Hall. **Grace Episcopal Church** (1847) has three, and two by Holman Hunt, another pioneer of the art glass movement. Further afield, you'll find Tiffanys in **Flatbush Reformed Dutch** (see p. 69), and in the Underwood chapel of **Lafayette Avenue Presbyterian Church** in Fort Greene, where the three-paneled landscape with mauve hills, a stream, trees, and luminous irises is as classic a Tiffany as you'll find anywhere.

★ America's oldest stained-glass windows were made by William Jay Bolton in 1844–48 for **St. Ann's Church** on Montague Street. Recently restored, they have deep, jewel-like colors; the overall effect is spectacular.

Brooklyn Heights
First Unitarian Church, *50 Monroe Place*, *718-624-5466*

First Presbyterian Church, *124 Henry Street, 718-624-3770*

Plymouth Church of the Pilgrims, *75 Hicks Street, 718-624-4743*

Grace Episcopal Church, *254 Hicks Street, 718-624-1850*

St. Ann's & the Holy Trinity Church, *157 Montague Street, 718-875-6960*
Subway: 2, 3, 4, 5 to Borough Hall

Flatbush
Flatbush Reformed Dutch Church, *890 Flatbush Avenue, 718-284-5140*
Subway: D, Q to Church Avenue

Fort Greene
Lafayette Avenue Presbyterian Church, *85 S. Oxford Street, 718-625-7515*
Subway: A to Lafayette Avenue: D, Q, 2, 3, 4, 5, to Atlantic Avenue

A Coffee Shop for All Seasons:
TOM'S RESTAURANT

What's an old luncheonette decorated with tinsel, artificial flowers, and wax fruit doing in this book? It isn't the best restaurant in Brooklyn, or the cheapest, or the most famous. It isn't even open for dinner—just breakfast and lunch. But Tom's is worth a visit, *many* visits, not only for its now rare cherry-lime rickies, excellent brisket, crisp bacon, and first-class egg salad, but because it embodies Brooklyn at its best—inclusive, kindly, and sustaining in more ways than one.

Tom's has been on Washington Avenue since 1936, just a few blocks from the Brooklyn Museum of Art and Botanic Garden. It's a hardscrabble neighborhood with few shops and virtually no other restaurants. Here, Tom's is a beloved institution. Such is the affection in which the place is held that during the '68 riots following the assassination of Martin Luther King, locals formed a human chain around Tom's to protect it from looters.

At lunch, counter and tables are filled with families, cops, nuns, office workers, and the occasional writerly type from Park Slope brooding over a laptop. The waitresses fuss over you with just the right degree of solicitude; the iced tea they bring is garnished with fresh mint. Meanwhile, Gus Vlahavas, son of the original Tom, presides with a beatific grin, a genuine interest in the contentment of his customers, and a relaxed sweetness with kids ("Have a candy for the journey home!"). Hanging on the tchotchke-bedecked walls, you'll find dozens of framed articles about Tom's, and in almost every one Gus is called "the friendliest man in Brooklyn." It's true!

Tom's Restaurant
782 Washington Avenue, 718-636-9738
Prospect Heights

★ Two other favorites: **Hinsch's** in Bay Ridge is bright and welcoming, and the waitresses are likely to call you "sweetie." The clientele includes retirees, young moms with their babies, and famished ladies in recovery after shopping on bustling 86th Street. Hinsch's does all the classics well: tuna salad, open turkey sandwich, rice pudding. The ice cream is made on the premises and is something special. In Park Slope, the new **Dizzy's** is an only- in-New-York kind of place, in that the owners graduated from the Culinary Institute of America and have devoted themselves to making the best corned beef hash, burgers, etc., you could imagine. The setting is sweetly hip, everyone is friendly, and all the ingredients of your meal—from the baby spinach to the extraordinary Lopez Bakery bread—are of the best quality.

Hinsch's Confectionery
8518 Fifth Avenue, 718-748-2854
Bay Ridge
Subway: R to 86th Street
Dizzy's
511 9th Street, 718-499-1966
Park Slope
Subway: F to Seventh Avenue

Spanning the Narrows:
VERRAZANO-NARROWS BRIDGE

When the Verrazano-Narrows Bridge opened in 1964, it was the longest suspension bridge in the world. It is immense—4,260 feet, to be precise. The towers are seventy stories high and slighter further apart at the top than at the bottom, because of the curvature of the earth. Still, it appears remarkably delicate. In the words of its designer, Othmar H. Ammann, it is "an enormous object drawn as faintly as possible." The

bridge is the first sight of New York City for ships entering New York harbor and for the thousands of runners who thunder across its graceful span at the start of the New York Marathon. Some runners report that they can feel the whole thing vibrating under the massed footfalls, but they have nothing to fear because the bridge's four steel-wire suspension cables measure a yard around each and they are affixed to massive concrete anchorages sunk deep into the ground. Still nervous? Both ends of the bridge are protected by the nation: Fort Wadsworth on the Staten Island side (where marathoners assemble before the starting gun) is now part of a national park; Fort Hamilton in Brooklyn is an Army base. There's more to the bridge than its size and beauty, though:

* It's home to a population of peregrine falcons, a species almost wiped out in the '70s. Evidently, the traffic noise doesn't outweigh the advantages of blustery winds (good for flying), plentiful pigeons, and flat, inaccessible nesting locales.

* Shore Park, the narrow strip of green between the Shore Parkway (aka the Belt Parkway) and the water, is beloved of joggers, bikers, bladers, skateboarders, and people who just like to sit on a bench

and enjoy the view. It was on one of the benches north of the bridge that John Travolta told Karen Lynn Gorney of his dreams in *Saturday Night Fever*. Incidentally, Travolta's story about the Verrazano construction worker who fell and remains embedded in the concrete is absolutely not true—but try telling that to any local aficionado. East of the bridge, along the edge of Gravesend Bay, the park widens a bit, forming one of the city's finest kite-flying locations.

* In Brooklyn, but technically not of it (it's federal land), is Fort Hamilton. On weekday afternoons, you can visit the tiny but fascinating **Harbor Defense Museum**, housed in a nineteenth-century bombproof building called a caponier (it means "chicken coop" in French).

* In contrast to the mighty Verrazano, the **Carroll Street Bridge** over the Gowanus Canal is tiny—only 45.2 feet at its widest—but it's the oldest retractile bridge (meaning that it slides aside on a track) in the country, dating from 1889.

> **Verrazano-Narrows Bridge,** *Bay Ridge*
> *Subway: R to Bay Ridge/95th Street*
>
> **Harbor Defense Museum,** *Fort Hamilton*
> *Fort Hamilton Parkway at 101st Street*
> *718-630-4349*
> *Car: Exit the Shore Parkway at Bay 8th Street*
>
> **Carroll Street Bridge,** *Gowanus*
> *Carroll Street between Bond and Nevins Streets*
> *Subway: F or G to Carroll Street; M, N or R*
> *to Union Street*

High Ideals, Low Rents:
WARREN PLACE
and Other Housing by
Alfred Tredway White

On Warren Place in Cobble Hill, forty-four elaborately ornamented, compact brick houses sit on either side of a private pedestrian mews, with gardens and a lily pond along the middle. Each end of the mews is anchored by two larger houses. This extraordinarily peaceful and beautiful place was built in 1879 to house workmen and their families. Now it's one of the most sought-after blocks in Brooklyn. The **Warren Place Workingmen's Cottages** were the project of Alfred Tredway White, a Victorian businessman whose favorite saying was "Philanthropy plus five percent," meaning, you can house people at an affordable price and still make a profit.

Just round the corner, on Hicks Street, are two other examples of White's imaginative constructions. The striking **Tower** and **Home** buildings on Hicks Street, at Baltic and Warren Streets, contain 226 low-rent apartments, designed with outside spiral staircases and balconies to allow for floor-through, well-ventilated apartments. In addition, they have garden courtyards, basement laundries, and—oh, joy!—a kitchen in each apartment, radical for the times. They must have seemed like

heaven then. Now, with their dark-red brick and ornate ironwork, they still look like wonderful places to live.

★ Only one more example of White's work survives—the **Riverside Apartments**, in Brooklyn Heights, at the corner of Columbia Place and Joralemon Street. Once they did stand by the river's side, but then the Brooklyn-Queens Expressway arrived and sliced off one side and the central garden.

> **Warren Place**, *146–154 Warren Street between Hicks and Henry Streets*
> **Tower Buildings**, *417–435 Hicks Street*
> **Home Buildings**, *439–445 Hicks Street*
> *Subway: F to Bergen Street*

Ghost Village:
WEEKSVILLE HOUSES

They appear like a mirage: four small wood-frame houses, sitting on an impeccable lawn in the shadow of the drab Kingsborough Houses. They are the only known vestiges of Weeksville, a thriving, free-black community of the nineteenth century. The street they lined was originally an Indian trail, then a colonial road down which Washington and his troops passed in 1776. These little buildings exude history, even when viewed through the chicken-wire fence that constitutes the Hunterfly Road Historic Houses of Weeksville's security system.

Named for James Weeks, a black stevedore who bought the land from the Lefferts family in 1838, Weeksville appears on maps and in newspapers as early as 1846. It was a calm and comfortable community. Susan Smith-McKinney, the first black female physician in New York State, was born here, as was Moses P. Cobb, Brooklyn's first black cop. Weeksville was a haven for runaway slaves as well as Manhattan blacks fleeing white mobs during the draft riots of 1863. By the 1880s, European immigration and the Brooklyn Bridge had changed Weeksville; its boundaries remained, but it was no longer distinctly black. By the 1960s, Weeksville existed only in the memories of a few old folks.

In 1968, a professor and a pilot who were looking for traces of Weeksville flew over the area and noticed a group of houses on a small curving lane (Old Hunterfly Road) that bore no relation to the modern grid system. The houses had been scheduled for demolition, to make way for more housing projects, but community action saved them. Joan Maynard, the gently determined director of Weeksville, recalls, "The children raised $975, the first money. You can't take money from poor little kids and not try your best. All the energy came from little children. They said, 'Let's fix up the old houses on Bergen Street and make it a history museum.'"

It happened. Oral remembrances of Weeksville have been recorded; more artifacts have been excavated from the site and donated than it has room to show. One of the houses has been turned into a classroom for lectures and indoor activities; another is a museum which frames the story of Weeksville around exhibits of clothing, furniture, even—grimly—a set of leg irons. Adjacent to the site, a large community garden is maintained by Kingsborough residents.

Weeksville has survived without government subsidy and with precious little philanthropic help. It has recently been awarded a grant from the Borough of Brooklyn, but it remains a grassroots preservation effort, by and for its community. There are no regular hours, but you can make an appointment to see it. Visit this extraordinary place, and when you're there it would be appropriate to make a donation.

Weeksville Houses
Old Hunterfly Road
1698 Bergen Street, Crown Heights
718-756-5250
Subway: 3, 4 to Utica Avenue

The Artists Have Arrived:
WILLIAMSBURG

Traditionally, forgotten or forlorn New York neighborhoods are discovered and revitalized by artists. In Brooklyn, it's happened to Williamsburg. Contrary to what you may have read, this place is not yet Soho. It is still irretrievably Brooklyn, and some of those black-clad figures darting around are not postmodernists—they are Hasidim.

Williamsburg has been an artists' outpost for years—cheap loft space, lots of sky, and (amazing but true) an easy subway ride into Manhattan. To get the feel, take the L train from Union Square to Bedford Street. It's only one stop into Brooklyn, but when you get out, you'll know you've arrived, as you look around at the hodgepodge of nineteenth- century houses and small manufacturing buildings. You'll also notice a funkily gentrifying main street bustling with cafes, bars, music stores, and antique shops.

The area that currently constitutes the happening drag is small: Bedford Street between N. 5th and N. 9th Streets. Pick up a copy of the *Waterfront Weekly* for gallery information; stop somewhere for coffee. Favorites are the hip but low-key **L Cafe**, and **Kasia's**, which offers tasty Polish and diner food in a log-cabinesque setting. The galleries are somewhat ad hoc at this point; the best way to keep track of them is by watching for listings of shows. **The Williamsburg Art and Historical Center** offers an eclectic mix of art shows, lectures, movies, concerts, and readings. The most appealing gallery has to be **Holland Tunnel**, an 8'-by-10' shed bought at Home Depot and featuring art and occasional performances.

You won't find Bruce Willis' latest at the **Ocularis** film series, held at **Gala-pagos**. More likely on offer will be something by Godard or Buñuel, which seems appropriate for a $5

WILLIAMSBURG
1$ PER
Sq. Ft. LOFT
VRS 25$
in SoHo

show on a Sunday night in a former mayonnaise facto-ry. Galapagos has a full bar and also presents theatre and art events. Favored hangouts of the moment are the mellow **Teddy's** (see p. 17) and the **Brooklyn Ale House** (for serious beer). **The Brooklyn Brewery** is a fascinating place, and you can get a look at the brew-ing process on the Saturday afternoon tours (free! with samples!). Locals like to go on Friday nights when it's open for happy hour.

Get here soon. It's changing week by week, which could mean that Smith & Hawken looms.

⋆ For good food in a bohemian setting, try **Oznot's Dish**, where a quirky sensibility meets Middle Eastern cuisine and there's a nice garden; **Plan Eat Thailand** for some of the city's best Thai food, and **Seasons**, a small, sweet bistro. For Mexican food and margaritas, check out **Vera Cruz** (see p. 100) or **Bean**, where the Mexican food has a vege-tarian slant (and you can also get takeout).
⋆ Also in Williamsburg, **Domsey's Clothing Warehouse** (p. 45) and the **Landmarks Preservation Commission Salvage Warehouse** (p. 91)

> **Bean**, *167 Bedford Avenue, 718-387-8222*
> **Brooklyn Ale House**, *103 Berry Street,*
> *718-302-9811*
> **Brooklyn Brewery**, *79 N. 11th Street,*
> *718-486-7422*
> **Holland Tunnel**, *62 S. 3rd Street, 718-384-5738*
> **Kasia's Restaurant**, *146 Bedford Avenue,*
> *718-387-8780*

L Cafe, *189 Bedford Avenue, 718-388-6792*
Ocularis/Galapagos, *70 N. 6th Street,*
718-388-8713
Oznot's Dish, *79 Berry Street, 718-599-6596*
Plan Eat Thailand, *184 Bedford Avenue,*
718-599-5758
Seasons, *556 Driggs Avenue, 718-384-9695*
Williamsburg Art & Historical Center,
135 Broadway, 718-963-1150/486-7372
Subway: L to Bedford Avenue

People Who Will Help You Find Out More about Brooklyn:
THE ENTHUSIASTS

So many people are devoted to studying Brooklyn, or
their corner of it, that it's hard to know where to
begin. Every community, from Gravesend to Green-
point, has a historical society or some equivalent. You
can tour almost any part of the borough, or check in
on one of the many Websites, which offer information
on everything from the efforts to save the Lott House
to the best General Tso's Chicken in the borough. This
listing is a start.

NB: All URLs are subject to change. Remember,
we warned you!

Information and Tours
**Brooklyn Center for the Urban Environment
(BCUE)**. The Tennis House, Prospect Park, 718-788-

8500. This energetic group is devoted to educating New Yorkers about their city. Under its benevolent aegis you can take all kinds of interesting tours—the Gowanus Canal (see p. 104), Immigrant Williamsburg, the Brooklyn Waterfront.

Tours of Hasidic Crown Heights with Rabbi Beryl Epstein, 718-953-5244 or 1-800-838-TOUR. This may be the only way to get a look inside the Hasidic world.

Brooklyn Information & Culture, 718-855-7882. Formerly the Fund for the Borough of Brooklyn, this group oversees events such as Welcome Back to Brooklyn and Celebrate Brooklyn, publishes *Meet Me in Brooklyn* (a quarterly calendar of events) and a Visitors' Guide. It's also the home of the **Brooklyn Tourism Council** (also 718-855-7882), which includes in its tour schedule a visit to African-American historic sites (call Braggin' about Brooklyn, 718-297-5107).

Brooklyn Historical Society, 718-624-0890. A trove of Brooklyn information and memorabilia. The society has been closed for a lengthy renovation; call to find out when it reopens.

New York Apple Tours (Brooklyn bus), 212-944-9200. Newly started, this tour bus takes in selected sights, including the Heights, Fulton Landing, the Brooklyn Museum of Art, Botanic Garden, some shopping, and cheesecake at Junior's.

Brooklyn Attitude Tours, 718-398-0939. Elliot Niles's bus-and-walking tour is designed to give a sampling of several different landmarks, neighborhoods, and cultures.

92nd Street Y, 212-996-1100. Offers some unusual tours: Jewish Williamsburg, Seagate, Brighton Beach, the Navy Yard, etc.

Free Shuttle Bus Service

In summer, the free **"A Day in Brooklyn"** trolley runs between the Brooklyn Botanic Garden, the Brooklyn Museum of Art, the Main Public Library, Prospect Park, and the Zoo. The bus runs every hour from noon to 5 P.M. on weekends and holidays. Call the Info-line at 718-965-8999.

The **"Trolley Express"** runs every half-hour between Grand Army Plaza and the Brooklyn Children's Museum, with a stop at the Brooklyn Museum of Art. Call the Children's Museum Hot Line at 718-735-4400.

Books, a Magazine, and the Library

Seeing New York by Hope Cooke (Temple University Press): Cooke is a marvelously erudite enthusiast and she lives in Brooklyn. Consequently, her sections about the borough are tender as well as informative.

AIA Guide to New York City by Eliot Wilensky and Norval White (Harcourt Brace Jovanovich): Opinionated, passionate, and essential for anyone who loves to explore the city.

Brooklyn's Green-Wood Cemetery by Jeffrey Richman (The Green-Wood Cemetery): Richman is the cemetery's tour guide par excellence. If these stones could speak, it would be with Richman's voice.

Brooklyn Bridge is a good-looking, always informative monthly magazine that's been in existence since September 1995. Good listings, nice photography. Look for it at any newsstand.

The Brooklyn Collection at the main branch of the Brooklyn Public Library contains books and documents, some of them very old. If the smart and helpful people here can't find what you're looking for (unlikely), they will know where it is. Call 718-230-2100 for hours.

Websites

Brooklyn Online, *www.brooklynonline.com*
Lots of wonderful historical essays, photos and links.

Pratt Institute, *www.pratt.edu*
Very pretty site, good pics of the steam engine and, best of all, the Pratt-cam!

Brooklyn Dodgers' Home Plate
www.brooklyn-dodgers.com For lovers of Dem Bums.

The General Tso's Chicken Survey
www.echonyc.com/~jkarpf/home/tales2.html
Everything you wanted to know about General Tso.

Park Slope Food Coop
www.people-link.com/users/foodcoop
The Coop's own site—straight ahead, informative.
http://www.echonyc.com/~jkarpf/home/tales2.html
Josh Karpf's Tales from the Coop—eccentric, amusing.

Brooklyn Tourism Council, *www.brooklynx.org*
Links to the Websites of cultural, tourist, and neighborhood groups.

Lesbian Herstory Archive
http://www.datalounge.net/network/pages/lha//

Selections from current exhibits and more.

Brooklyn Public Library

http://www.brooklynpubliclibrary.org/

Very useful, with lots of links to other sites.

Brooklyn Museum of Art, *www.Brooklynart.org*

Very basic.

Brooklyn Botanic Garden, *www.bbg.org* Ditto.

Prospect Park Alliance, *www.prospectpark.org*

Comprehensive listing of places and events, with photographs.

Aquarium for Wildlife Conservation *www.wcs.org*

Good for events listings.

Coney Island, *www.coneyislandusa.com*

Ebullient guide to the freaks and sights, with links to more.

Database of People Born in Brooklyn *www.didax-ts.com*

Brooklyn Bridge Live Camera

http://www.romdog.com/bridge/brooklyn.html

A quick look a day keeps the doctor away.

WILLIAMSBURG BRIDGE
GREEN-Point
MANHATTAN BRIDGE
Williamsburg
QUEENS
BROOKLYN
DUMBO
Bedford-Stuyvesant
Pratt
FORT GREENE
DOWN TOWN
Brooklyn HEIGHTS
Atlantic avenue
Prospect HEIGHTS
Carroll GARDENS
GOWANUS
WEEKSVILLE HOUSES
Crown HEights
PARK SLOPE
PROSPECT Park
FLATBUSH AVENUE
Green-Wood Cemetery
FLATBUSH
gateway NATIONAL RECREATION area
Bensonhurst
GRAVESEND
Sheepshead Bay
Brighton beach
CONEY Island
Atlantic Ocean

Acknowledgments

We have been helped by many people in the preparation of this book. We thank them for the gifts of their time and their expertise. Any factual errors in these pages are ours alone.

Melisa Coburn of City & Company

Joan Arnold

Arthur Boehm

John Buskin

Betsy Carter

Kate Altman

Richard H. Drucker of the Brooklyn Navy Yard Development Corporation

Chris Ricciardi

Ed Carter of the Fort Greene Youth Patrol

Joan Maynard of the Society for the Preservation of Weeksville and Bedford-Stuyvesant History

Christine Mark and Barbara McTiernan of the Prospect Park Alliance

Jack Kleinsinger

Arnold J. Smith

Jeff Richman

Edith Bartley at Plymouth Church of the Pilgrims

Ron McFarlin at the Unitarian Church

Vera Beaudin Saeedpour of the Kurdish Museum

William Jordan at Siloam Presbyterian Church

Stan Murray

David Sharps of the Hudson Waterfront Museum

Alix Friedman of the 92nd Street YMHA

Sally Williams of The Brooklyn Museum of Art

Aldona Rygelis

Roger Rosenthal

Chris MacManus

Ken Emerson

Amanda Sutphin of the Landmarks Preservation
Commission

Marien Lo Preto

JoAnne Meyers of Brooklyn Information and Culture

Toby Brandt and Dan Wiley of Brooklyn Center for the
Urban Environment

NEIGHBORHOOD INDEX

Atlantic Avenue

Atlantic Avenue Tunnel 120
Brawta 62
Breukelen (& Bark) 49
Jerry Johnson 104
Montero's Bar & Grill 16
Olde Good Things 91
Peter's Ice Cream Cafe 85
Sahadi Importing Co. 125
Time Trader Antiques 91

Bay Ridge

Century 21 45
Harbor Defense
    Museum 87,133
Hinsch's Confectionery
    84,130
Kleinfelds 45
Leske's Bakery 64
Nordic Delicacies 64
Norwegian-American
17th of May Parade 33
Pho Hoai 64
Revolutionary War
    Cemetery 77
Shore Park 86, 132
T. J. Bentley's 100
Verrazano-Narrows
    Bridge 131

Bedford-Stuyvesant

Concord Baptist Church 19
Magnolia Tree Earth
    Center 95
McCafe 63

Bensonhurst/ Bath Beach

Christmas Lights 18
Feast of Santa Rosalia 18
Nellie Bly
    Amusement Park 85

Brighton Beach

Cafe Restaurant Volna 22
Cafe Tatiana 22
Classic Galleria 23
Golden Key 23
M & I 23
Magic Corsets 23
Mrs. Stahl's Knishery 24
Odessa 23
Primorski 101
Rasputin 101
Sea Lane Bakery 23
Winter Garden 101

Brooklyn Heights

Brooklyn Heights
    Promenade 78
First Presbyterian
    Church 128

First Unitarian Church 127
Garden Place 35
Grace Court 35
Grace Episcopal Church 128
Pierrepont Playground 87
Herman Behr House 35
Hicks Street 36
Middagh Street 36
Montero's Bar and Grill 16
New York Transit
 Museum 86
Plymouth Church
 of the Pilgrims 36
Riverside Apartments 135
64 Poplar Street 15
St. Ann's Church 128
St Mark's Comics 84
Tango 46
Willow Place 35
Willow Street 35

Carroll Gardens

Astroturf 92
Caputo's 43
D'Amico Foods 44
Dave's 5 & 10 43
Helen's Place 43
John Rankin residence 43
Monteleone's 44
Painted Pot 84
P. J. Hanley's 16
Sinatra's Museum Caffe
 Nostalgia and Coo
 Coo Nest 43

Cobble Hill

Brooklyn Artisans
 Gallery 50
Shakespeare's Sister 92
Home Buildings 134
Tower Buildings 134
Warren Place Workingmen's
 Cottages 134

Coney Island

Astroland 85
B & B Carousell 48
Coney Island Sewage
 Treatment Plant 103
Coney Island USA 48
Cyclone 48
Deno's 85
Faber's Arcade 48
Mermaid Day Parade 33
Nathan's Famous
 Restaurant 48, 59
New York Aquarium 87, 89,
 98, 144
Parachute Jump 48
Philip's Candy Store 47
Polar Bears 33
Ruby's Old
 Thyme Bar 17, 48
Sideshows by
 the Seashore 48
Steeplechase Pier 68
Thunderbolt 48
Tiltawhirl 48

Crown Heights

Brooklyn Children's
  Museum 86
Tours of Hasidic Crown
  Heights 141
Weeksville Houses 135

Downtown

City of Brooklyn Fire
  Headquarters 106
Dime Savings Bank 106
Gage and Tollner 56
Junior's 58
Urban Glass 51

Dumbo/Fulton Landing

Anchorage 13, 53
Art Under the Bridge 53
Bargemusic 14
Creative Time 53
Eagle Warehouse 106
Fulton Ferry Cafe 15
Grimaldi's Pizzeria 53
River Cafe 60

Eastern Parkway

Brooklyn Botanic Garden 27
Brooklyn Museum of Art 36
Chili Pepper Festival 28
Sakura Matsuri Cherry
  Blossom Festival 28
West Indian Day Parade 30

Flatbush

Brooklyn Center at
  Brooklyn College 90

Buzz-a-rama 74
Erasmus Hall High
  School 70
Flatbush Reformed Dutch
  Church 69
Flatlands Dutch Reformed
  Church 70
Kenmore and Albemarle
  Terraces 70
Loew's Kings Theater 70
S&W 45
Train World 121

Fort Greene

Brooklyn Academy of Music
  (BAM) 25
Brooklyn Navy Yard 39
Cambodian Cuisine 26
Fort Greene Park 15
Joseph Steele House 114
Lafayette Avenue
  Presbyterian Church
  114, 128
Miss Ann's 114
New City Bar and Grill 26, 61
99 Ryerson Street 15
Prison Ship Martyrs'
  Monument 113
Reliable & Franks Naval
  Uniforms 41
South Portland Street 114
Williamsburgh Savings
  Bank Tower 105

Gateway National Recreation Area

Canarsie Pier 67
Dead Horse Bay 67
Floyd Bennett Field 71, 89
Gateway Golf & Tennis
   Range 86

Gowanus

Carroll Street Bridge 133
Gowanus Canal Tour 104
Monte's Italian Restaurant 59

Grand Army Plaza

Brooklyn Public Library
   107, 143, 144
Greenmarket 117
Soldiers' and Sailors'
   Memorial Arch 115

Gravesend

Old Gravesend Cemetery 77
Lady Deborah Moody/
   Van Sicklen House 55

King's Highway

Mabat 63

Marine Park/ Mill Basin

Brennan and Carr 56
Dutch Houses 53
Gil Hodges Lanes 73
Jamaica Bay Riding
   Academy 89

Let's-watch-the-horseshoe-
   crabs-mating walk 72
Mill Basin Kosher Deli and
   Fine Art Gallery 102

Park Slope

Barnes & Noble 110
Blum County 92, 110
Brooklyn Tabernacle 21
Brownstone Billiards 74
Carroll Street 110
Christie's Jamaican
   Patties 62
Clay Play 84
Clay Pot 50
Community Bookstore 109
Comics Plus 84
Cucina 59
Dizzy's 84, 131
Flux & Co. 92
Gowanus Arts Exchange 84
Hooti Couture 108
John Morisi and Sons 110
Last Exit Books 110
Leaf 'n' Bean 108
Lesbian Herstory
   Archive 97, 143
Little Things 109
Lucky Bug 90
Luna Park 85, 88
Max and Moritz 61
Montgomery Place 110
Mostly Modern 92, 110
New Prospect at Home 111
Old Stone House 87, 89
Park Slope Food Coop
   108, 143

Pavilion Theatre 86
Puppetworks 88
Spoke the Hub Dancing 84
Stanley's Place 83
Two Boots 87
Zuzu's Petals 108

Pratt Campus Area
Pratt Institute's Engine
  Room 32, 111, 143

Prospect Heights
Kurdish Library and
  Museum 96
Tom's Restaurant 84, 129
Up Over Cafe 101

Prospect Park
Brooklyn Center for the
  Urban Environment
  (BCUE) 140
Camperdown Elm 117
Celebrate Brooklyn 29
Imagination Playground
  87, 89
Kensington Stables 89
Lefferts Homestead
  Children's Museum
  56, 88, 89, 116
Long Meadow 115
Park Rangers 87
Pedal Boats 88
Prospect Lake 68
Prospect Park Alliance
  117, 144

Prospect Park Annual
  Fishing Contest 68
Prospect Park Wildlife
  Center 88, 89, 90
Quaker Cemetery 116
Sheep Meadow 86
Soldiers' and Sailors'
  Memorial Arch 115
Uncle Luigi's 85
Welcome Back to Brooklyn
  Homecoming Festival 29
Wollman Rink 89
You Gotta Have Park 29

Red Hook
Beard Street Pier 122
Brooklyn Clay Retort &
  Firebrick Works 123
Hudson Waterfront Museum
  89, 97, 123, 124
Lehigh Valley Barge 89, 123
Red Hook Yacht and
  Kayak Club 16, 124

Sheepshead Bay
Bernie's Fishing Tackle 66
Blessing of the Fleet 32
Dorothy B. 66
Enrico Caruso Museum
  of America 96
Fishing 65
Flamingo III 66
Funtime USA 83
Loehmann's 45
Lundy Brothers 58
Pho Hoai 64
Sea Queen IV 66

Sunset Park

Green-Wood Cemetery 75
McGovern Weir 77
Melody Lanes 83
Pho Hoai 64

Williamsburg/ Greenpoint

Bean 139
Brooklyn Ale House 139
Brooklyn Brewery 139
Domsey's Warehouse 45, 139
Galapagos 138
Giglio 30
Holland Tunnel 138
Kasia's Restaurant 138
L Cafe 138
Landmarks Preservation
  Commission Architectural
  Salvage Warehouse 91,139

Metropolitan Pool 89
Ocularis 138
Oznot's Dish 139
Peter Luger Steakhouse 57
Plan Eat Thailand 139
R 92
Russian Orthodox Cathedral
  of the Transfiguration 24
Seasons 139
Teddy's 17, 139
Ugly Luggage 92
Vera Cruz 100, 139
Watching the July 4th fire-
  works in Greenpoint 34
Williamsburg Art and
  Historical Center 138
Williamsburgh Savings Bank
  106

GENERAL INDEX

Admiral's Row 41
AIA Guide to New York City
  142
Amusement arcades 83
Anchorage 13, 53
Art Under the Bridge 53
Astroland 85
Astroturf 92
Atlantic Antic 30
Atlantic Avenue 91
Atlantic Avenue Tunnel 120
B & B Carousell 48, 84
Bargemusic 14

Barnes & Noble 110
Baseball artifacts 83
Bean 139
Beard Street Pier 122
Bedford-Stuyvesant 82
Bensonhurst 18
Bernie's Fishing Tackle 66
Black Cowboys 103
Blessing of the Fleet 32
Bloom-Stoothoff House 55
Blum County 92, 110
Boerum Hill 82
Bowling 83

Brawta 62

Brennan and Carr 56

Breukelen (& Bark) 49

Brighton Beach 22

Broadway Junction-East
  New York elevated
  subway stop 120

Brooklyn Academy of Music
  (BAM) 25, 90

Brooklyn Ale House 139

Brooklyn Artisans
  Gallery 50

Brooklyn Attitude Tours 141

Brooklyn Botanic Garden
  27, 85, 144

Brooklyn Brewery 139

Brooklyn Bridge 142

Brooklyn Bridge 12

Brooklyn Bridge Live
  Camera 13, 144

Brooklyn Center at
  Brooklyn College 90

Brooklyn Center for the
  Urban Environment
  (BCUE) 140

Brooklyn Children's
  Museum 86

Brooklyn Clay Retort &
  Firebrick Works 123

Brooklyn Collection 143

Brooklyn Dodgers' Home
  Plate 143

Brooklyn Heights 34
  Brooklyn Heights
  Promenade 78

Brooklyn Historic Railway
  Association 90, 120, 123

Brooklyn Historical
  Society 141

Brooklyn Information &
  Culture 141

Brooklyn Museum of Art
  36, 85, 144

Brooklyn Navy Yard 39

Brooklyn Online 143

Brooklyn Public Library
  107, 143, 149

Brooklyn Tabernacle 21

Brooklyn Tourism Council
  141, 143

Brooklyn Waterfront Artists
  Coalition (BWAC) 124

*Brooklyn's Green-Wood
  Cemetery* 142

Brownstone Billiards 74, 88

Buzz-a-rama 500 74, 89

Cafe Restaurant Volna 22

Cafe Tatiana 22

Cambodian Cuisine 26, 114

Camperdown Elm 117

Canarsie Pier 67

Caputo's 43

Carousels 88

Carroll Gardens 42, 92

Carroll Street 110

Carroll Street Bridge 133

Celebrate Brooklyn 29

Century 21 45

Chili Pepper Festival 28

Christie's Jamaican
  Patties 62

Christmas Lights 18
City of Brooklyn Fire
  Headquarters 106
Classic Galleria 23
Clay Play 84
Clay Pot 50, 109
Coffee shops 84
Comic bookstores 84
Comics Plus 84
Commandant's House 40
Community Bookstore 109
Concord Baptist Church 19
Coney Island 47, 144
Coney Island Sewage
  Treatment Plant 103
Coney Island USA 48
Crafts Shops 49, 84
Creative Time 53
Cucina 59
Cyclone 48
D'Amico Foods 44
Dance 84
"Day in Brooklyn, A" 142
Database of people born
  in Brooklyn 144
Dave's 5 & 10 43
Dead Horse Bay 67
Deno's 85
Dime Savings Bank 106
Dizzy's 84, 131
Domsey's Warehouse
  45, 139
Dorothy B. 66
Dumbo 52
Dutch Houses 53
Eagle Warehouse 106

Egyptian Mummy 85
Elias Hubbard Ryder House
  55, 56
Enrico Caruso
  Museum of America 96
Erasmus Hall High
  School 70
Faber's Arcade 48, 83
Feast of Santa Rosalia 18
First Presbyterian
  Church 128
First Unitarian Church 127
Fishing 65
Flamingo III 66
Flatbush 68
Flatbush Reformed Dutch
  Church 69, 128
Flatlands Dutch Reformed
  Church 70
Floyd Bennett Field 71, 89
Flux & Co. 92
Fort Greene 114
Fort Greene Park 15
Frank Freeman 35, 106
Fulton Ferry Cafe 15
Funfairs 85
Funtime USA 83
Gage and Tollner 56
Galapagos 138
Garden Place 35
Gateway Golf & Tennis
  Range 86
General Tso's Chicken
  Survey 143
Giant turtle 85
Giglio 30

Gil Hodges Lanes   73, 83

Golden Key   23

Gowanus Arts Exchange   84

Gowanus Canal   104

Gowanus Canal Tour   104

Grace Court   35

Grace Episcopal Church   128

Greenmarket   117

Green-Wood Cemetery   75

Grimaldi's Pizzeria   53, 88

Harbor Defense Museum
   87, 133

Hasidic Crown Heights   141

Helen's Place   43

Hendrick I. Lott House   54

Herman Behr House
   35, 106

Hicks Street   36

Hinsch's Confectionery
   84, 130

Holland Tunnel   138

Home Buildings   134

Hooti Couture   108

House Tours   80

Hudson Waterfront Museum
   89, 97, 123, 124

Imagination Playground
   87, 89

Jamaica Bay Riding
   Academy   89

Jan Martense Schenk
   House   55

Jerry Johnson   104

John Morisi and Sons   110

Johannes Van Nuyse/
   Coe House   54

John Rankin residence   43

Joseph Steele House   114

Junior's   58

Kasia's Restaurant   138

Kenmore and Albemarle
   Terraces   70

Kensington Stables   89

Kids   83, 90

Kids 'n Action   86

Kleinfelds   45

Kurdish Library and
   Museum   96

L Cafe   138

Lady Deborah Moody/
   Van Sicklen House   55

Lafayette Avenue
   Presbyterian Church
   114, 128

Landmarks Preservation
   Commission Architectural
   Salvage Warehouse
   91, 139

Last Exit Books   110

Leaf 'n' Bean   108

Lefferts Homestead
   Children's Museum
   56, 88, 89, 116

Lehigh Valley Barge   89, 123

Lesbian Herstory Archive
   97, 143

Leske's Bakery   64

Let's-watch-the-horseshoe-
   crabs-mating walk   72

Little Things   109

Loehmann's   45

Loew's Kings Theater   70

Long Meadow 115
Lucky Bug 90
Luna Park 85, 88
Lundy Brothers 58
M & I 23
Mabat 63
Magic Corsets 23
Magnolia Tree Earth
  Center 95
Manahata Indian
  Arts Council 88
Max and Moritz 61
McCafe 63
McGovern Weir 77
Melody Lanes 83
Mermaid Day Parade 33
Metropolitan Pool 89
Middagh Street 36
Mill Basin Kosher Deli and
  Fine Art Gallery 102
Miss Ann's 114
Monteleone's 44
Monte's Italian
  Restaurant 59
Montero's Bar and Grill 16
Montgomery Place 110
Mostly Modern 92, 110
Mrs. Stahl's Knishery 24
Museums 95
Nathan's Famous
  Restaurant 48, 59
Naval Hospital 40
Nellie Bly
  Amusement Park 85
New City Bar
  and Grill 26, 61

New Prospect at Home 111
New Years Eve at Pratt 32
New York Apple Tours 141
New York Aquarium
  87, 89, 98, 144
New York Transit
  Museum 86
99 Ryerson Street 15
92nd Street Y 141
Nordic Delicacies 64
Norwegian-American
  17th of May Parade 33
Ocularis 138
Odessa 23
Old Gravesend Cemetery 77
Old Stone House 87, 89, 105
Olde Good Things 91
Oznot's Dish 139
P. J. Hanley's 16
Painted Pot 84
Parachute Jump 48
Park Rangers 87
Park Slope 92, 107
Park Slope Food Coop
  108, 143
Parks programs 87
Parrots 102
Pavilion Theatre 86
Pedal Boats 88
Peter Luger Steakhouse 57
Peter's Ice Cream Cafe 85
Philip's Candy Store 47
Pho Hoai 64
Pierrepont Playground 87
Pieter Claesen Wyckoff
  House 54

Plan Eat Thailand   139

Plymouth Church
   of the Pilgrims   36, 128

Polar Bears, Coney
   Island   33

Pool   88

Powwows   88

Pratt Institute   32, 111, 143

Pratt Institute's Engine
   Room   111

Primorski   101

Prison Ship Martyrs'
   Monument   113

Prospect Heights   82

Prospect Lake   68

Prospect-Lefferts
   Gardens   82

Prospect Park   88, 115

Prospect Park Alliance
   117, 144

Prospect Park Annual
   Fishing Contest   68

Prospect Park Wildlife
   Center   88, 89, 90

Puppetworks   88

Quaker Cemetery   116

R   92

Rasputin   101

Red Hook   89, 121

Red Hook Yacht and
   Kayak Club   16, 124

Reliable & Franks
   Naval Uniforms   41

Revolutionary War
   Cemetery   77

River Cafe   60

Riverside Apartments   135

Ruby's Old
   Thyme Bar   17, 48

Russian nightclubs   101

Russian Orthodox Cathedral
   of the Transfiguration   24

Ryder-Van Cleef House   54

S&W   45

Sahadi Importing Co.   125

Sakura Matsuri Cherry
   Blossom Festival   28

Schenck (Stoothoff)-
   Williamson House   54

Scouting Party   90

Sea Lane Bakery   23

Sea Queen IV   66

Seasons   139

Seeing New York   142

Shakepeare's Sister   92

Sheepshead Bay   65

Shore Road Park   86, 132

Sideshows by
   the Seashore   48

Sinatra's Museum Caffe
   Nostalgia and Coo Coo
   Nest   43

64 Poplar Street   15

Soldiers' and Sailors'
   Memorial Arch   115

South Portland Street   114

Spoke the Hub Dancing   84

Spring Plant Sale   28

St. Ann's Church   128

St. Mark's Comics   84

Stanley's Place   83

Steeplechase Pier   68

Stoothoff-Baxter-
  Kouwenhoven House 56
T. J. Bentley's 100
Tango 46
Teddy's 17, 139
Thunderbolt 48
Tiffany windows 127
Tiltawhirl 48
Time Trader Antiques 91
Tom's Restaurant 84, 129
Tours of Brooklyn 140
Tower Buildings 134
Train World 121
Tree Grows in Brooklyn, A
  94
"Trolley Express" 142
Two Boots 87
Ugly Luggage 92
Uncle Luigi's 85
Up Over Cafe 101
Urban Glass 51
Van Nuyse-Magaw
  House 56
Van Pelt-Woolsey House 56
Vera Cruz 100, 139
Verrazano-Narrows
  Bridge 131

Victorian Flatbush 80
Walt Whitman 15
Warren Place Workingmen's
  Cottages 134
Watching July 4th fireworks
  in Greenpoint 34
Web sites 143
Weeksville Houses 135
Weirdo Novelty Shops 90
Welcome Back to Brooklyn
  Homecoming Festival 29
West Indian Day Parade 30
Williamsburg 91, 137
Williamsburg Art
  and Historical Center 138
Williamsburgh Savings
  Bank 106
Williamsburgh Savings
  Bank Tower 105
Willow Place 35
Willow Street 35
Winter Garden 101
Wollman Rink 89
Wyckoff-Bennett
  Homestead 55
You Gotta Have Park 29
Zuzu's Petals 108

About the Authors

Alfred Gingold and Helen Rogan have published numerous books and articles, including *The Cool Parents Guide to All of New York*. They live in Brooklyn (where else?) with their son.

About the Artist

Aaron Meshon graduated from the Rhode Island School of Design in 1995 and too hastily moved to Manhattan, only to miss out on the ample closet space and beef patties indigenous to Brooklyn.